the yarn girls' guide to kid knits

the yarn girls' guide to kid knits

patterns for babies and toddlers

JULIE CARLES AND JORDANA JACOBS

PHOTOGRAPHS BY ELLEN SILVERMAN

ILLUSTRATIONS BY DANIELLA COHN AND GAIL CADEN

CLARKSON POTTER / PUBLISHERS

NEW YORK

Published by Clarkson Potter/Publishers, New York, New York.

Member of the Crown Publishing Group, a division of Random House, Inc.

www.crownpublishing.com

www.clarksonpotter.com

CLARKSON N. POTTER is a trademark and POTTER
and colophon are registered trademarks of Random House, Inc.

Portions of this work previously appeared in *The Yarn Girls' Guide to Simple Knits*
(Clarkson Potter, 2002).

Printed in China

Design by Jan Derevjanik

Library of Congress Cataloging-in-Publication Data
Carles, Julie.
The yarn girls' guide to kid knits : patterns for babies and toddlers /
Julie Carles and Jordana Jacobs.—1st ed.
p.   cm.
1. Knitting—Patterns.   2. Infants' clothing.   I. Jacobs, Jordana.   II. Title.
TT825 .C18   2004
746.43'20432—dc22   2003018489

ISBN 1-4000-5171-1

10 9 8 7 6 5 4 3 2 1

First Edition

We dedicate this book to

Jeff, John,

Max,

and

Olivia.

acknowledgments

Thanks to all the adorable children that are photographed in this book: Nico, Matthew, Oscar, Max, Marley, Devan, David, Rena, Chase, Jonathan, Maya, Pilar, Luna, Sela, Demitri, and Olivia. Also many thanks to their parents, who took time out from their busy days to bring them to the studio. We would like to thank Ellen Silverman for the amazing photographs, as well as Alli and Skippy for all their help in the studio.

Our Yarn Company staff's hard work is much appreciated on a daily basis as well as with this book. We also want to thank Petra, Mercedes, and Tara for helping us knit everything. Rosy Ngo and Carla Glasser made this book possible. And finally we need to thank our customers, who inspired many of these designs.

Contents

introduction

Knitting for kids is both fun and rewarding. Knitted sweaters, blankets, hats, or any other items make great gifts—they are quick to knit, and the knitter feels accomplishment and pride because she or he has made something from the heart. The parents feel they have received a gift made with love—and the child gets to wear something cute, unique, and made just for him or her.

We had a wonderful response to our first book, *The Yarn Girls' Guide to Simple Knits*. People appreciated the simple styles that knit up quickly. A baby book using the same premise seemed like the next logical book for us to write—logical because we have both recently become new mothers. Jordana was first, with the arrival of Max in December 2002; then Julie gave birth to Olivia the following June. Although we have knit many, many baby items over the years, both as samples for the store and as gifts for our friends, these newest additions to our lives have inspired us further. They have also shown us the true *necessity* of knitting simple, fast projects that look adorable. Kid sweaters are always popular knitting projects at our store. The patterns we chose for this book are some of the favorites we have accumulated over the years. Customers—and the kids they knit for—have inspired many of the designs.

Although this book is based on the same premise as *The Yarn Girls' Guide to Simple Knits*, we have made a few changes. We knitted up two versions of each sweater, one for a boy and one for a girl. Some people see a sweater made in pink yarn and think the pattern will yield a girl's sweater only. They have a hard time envisioning it knit up in blue. We hope that seeing both versions will allow you to see that most sweater patterns are unisex—just changing the color makes a big difference. We also included additional color combinations where we thought a little extra visual would be helpful.

In this book, you will find easy-to-knit patterns for sweaters, blankets, hats, dresses, ponchos, and a bunting. All the designs are simple and use fun yarns. These patterns are perfect for the true beginner or for those who want immediate satisfaction and a project that requires mindless knitting. (We now know how important this is.) However, there are two Beyond Basic chapters with patterns that add a little something extra to the fundamental shapes. Sometimes we use color to add variety and other times just an interesting stitch to give the most basic sweater a little pizzazz. These are great opportunities for beginners to learn new techniques. When you want a little bit of a challenge, these sweaters are the perfect options.

The yarns we chose for the projects cover a range of gauges. The smallest gauge we use is 5 stitches per inch and the largest is about 1½ stitches per inch. The thinner yarns are more appropriate for younger babies. Don't worry; they still knit quickly because they are small items. And we didn't go too thin—the smallest needle we used is a 6. For sizes 1 year and older, we felt more comfortable using chunkier yarns because bigger kids can wear them with ease.

Finally, we want to remind you that this book has many resources for the new knitter. We have included a how-to-knit section that describes the fundamentals of knitting—all the techniques needed to complete any pattern in the book. We have also included a section of helpful hints. Here we offer you words of wisdom and general advice to help you avoid the pitfalls we come across daily. And last but not least, we have step-by-step directions to help you shape necklines and armholes (where applicable) and to aid in increasing in pattern on the sleeves.

We hope you enjoy these patterns as much as we do. Have fun, be creative—and happy knitting!

—JULIE AND JORDANA

the yarn girls' guide to the fundamentals

Has it been a long time since you picked up a pair of knitting needles? If so, you may be a bit rusty on the rudiments. Face it, we all get confused and forget things we have learned—even if we just learned them yesterday. Our goals are to make knitting as easy as possible and to enable you to create a sweater—start to finish—without a million trips to your local knitting store or tears and frustration. This chapter provides instructions on the basic techniques we use throughout the book. If you are a new knitter, or if you're a bit out of practice, this is where you'll turn for directions on how to knit, purl, cast on, and bind off. If you have forgotten how to make a slip knot or do a rib stitch, if you're not sure how to increase, decrease, or bind off, or can't quite recall any of the other fundamental tools for making a knitted garment, you're in the right place. And whether this is a refresher course or your first foray into the pleasures of knitting, we promise to keep it simple.

By the way, for you lefties out there, don't be intimidated. These directions are universal, and we teach righties and lefties to knit exactly the same way. If, however, you feel you want to alter the motions slightly to compensate, go ahead—just do what feels comfortable for you.

You may also have seen or heard about the European method of knitting, in which you knit with yarn wrapped around your left index finger to make a new stitch rather than wrapping the yarn around the needle with the right hand. All the illustrations and instructions in this book are based on the American method, which is how we knit and what we teach our students. If you already know how to knit in the European method, continue to do so if that's what you're comfortable with—these patterns will work equally well for you. Just make extra sure your gauge is correct.

SLIP KNOT AND CAST ON

Even before you begin to knit, you must cast the necessary number of stitches onto your needle. To do this, you have to measure out a length of yarn for a "tail," which will become your cast-on stitches. The length of the tail determines how many stitches you can cast on; the more stitches you are casting on, the longer the tail must be. Our rule of thumb is that an arm's length—that is, the distance from your wrist to your shoulder—of yarn will yield 20 stitches on the needle. So, if you need to cast on 100 stitches, you'll need to use 5 arm lengths of yarn. It is always better to have too long a tail than too short. If your tail runs out before you have cast on the required number of stitches, you will have to start over with a longer tail. You can always cut the remaining yarn off if the tail is too long, but always leave at least 2 or 3 inches.

After you measure out the tail, make a slip knot, which will also be your first cast-on stitch. Place this on a needle, hold that needle in your right hand, and continue to cast on stitches until you have the required number on the needle.

to make a slip knot

1. Measure out the required length of yarn and, with the free end hanging, make a loop at the measured point. You should see an *X*. (Illus. A)

2. Grab hold of the strand of yarn that is on the top of the *X* and bring this strand behind and through the loop. (Illus. B)

3. Hold this new loop in one hand and pull on the loose ends to create your slip knot! (Illus. C & D)

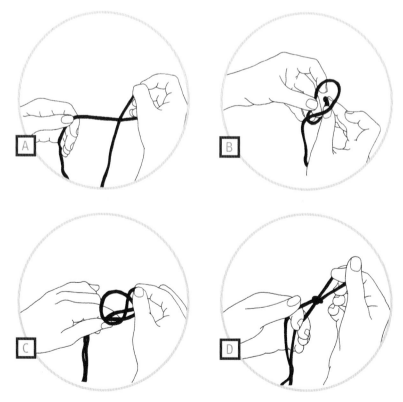

to cast on

1. Place your slip knot on a needle. Hold the needle in your right hand pointing toward the left. Hold the slip knot in place with your right index finger so it does not fly off the needle. (Illus. A)

2. Place the thumb and index finger of your left hand between the 2 strands of yarn dangling from the needle. (Your thumb should be closer to you and the index finger away from you.) Hold the dangling yarn taut with your ring and pinky fingers. (Illus. B)

3. Flip your left thumb up while guiding the needle down and to the left. A loop should form around your thumb. (Illus. C)

4. Guide the needle up through the loop on your thumb. Guide the needle over the yarn that is around your index finger and catch it with the needle. (Illus. D)

5. Guide the yarn hooked by the needle down through the loop around your thumb. (Illus. E and F) Slip your thumb out of its loop and place this thumb inside the strand of yarn that is closer to you. Pull down gently. Now you have a cast-on stitch!

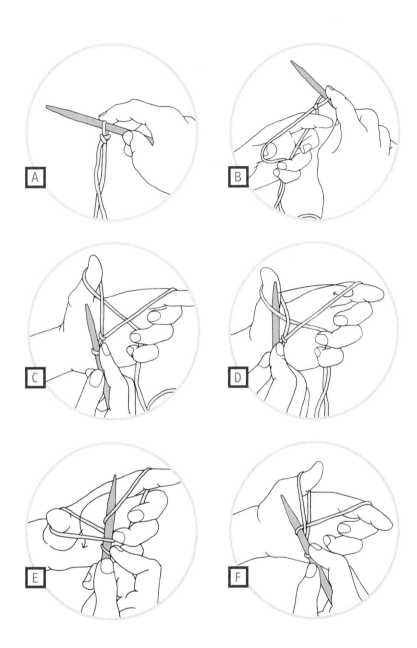

KNIT AND PURL

Knit and purl are the two stitches that make up the craft of knitting—everything else is merely a variation on one or both of these stitches. Once you master the knit and purl stitches, the world of knitting is yours to conquer.

to knit

1. Cast on the number of stitches required by your chosen pattern or 20 stitches if you are just practicing. Hold the needle with the cast-on stitches in your left hand and the empty needle in your right hand. Point the needles toward each other. (Illus. A)

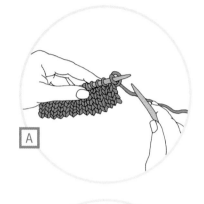

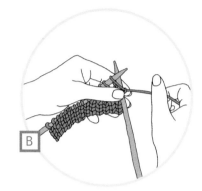

2. While holding the yarn in the back, insert the right needle from front to back through the first stitch on the left needle. You will see that the needles form an *X* with the right needle beneath the left needle. (Illus. B)

3. Keep the needles crossed by holding both needles with the thumb, index, and middle fingers of your left hand. Do this by holding the right needle with the thumbnail on top facing you and the nails of the index and middle fingers underneath that right needle and facing away from you. With your right hand, pick up the yarn and wrap it under and around the bottom needle; do not wrap it around the left needle. (Illus. C)

4. Hold the yarn in place around the right needle between your right thumb and index finger and guide the right needle toward you through the center of the stitch on the left needle. (Illus. D) The right needle should now be on top of the left needle. (Illus. E)

5. Pull the remaining yarn off the left needle by pulling the right needle up and to the right so the newly formed stitch slides off the left needle to the right. You will have a newly created stitch on the right needle. (Illus. F)

6. Repeat steps 1 through 5 across the entire row of stitches.

NOTE: WHEN YOU FINISH KNITTING THE ENTIRE ROW, ALL OF YOUR STITCHES WILL BE ON THE RIGHT NEEDLE. SWITCH HANDS, PLACING THE EMPTY NEEDLE IN YOUR RIGHT HAND AND THE NEEDLE WITH THE STITCHES ON IT IN YOUR LEFT HAND. NOW YOU ARE READY TO BEGIN KNITTING ANOTHER ROW.

to purl

1. Hold the needle with the stitches in your left hand and the empty needle in your right hand and the loose yarn hanging in front of your work. The needles should be pointed toward each other. (Illus. A)

2. Insert the right needle back to front through the front of the first stitch on the left needle. The needles will form an X with the right needle on top of the left needle. Make sure the yarn is in front of the needle. (Illus. B)

3. Keep the needles crossed in the X position by holding both needles with the thumb, index, and middle fingers of your left hand. Do this by holding the right needle with the thumbnail on top facing you and the nails of the index and middle fingers underneath that right needle and facing away. Wrap the yarn over and around the front needle from the back, bringing the yarn around and in front of the right needle. (Illus. C)

4. Holding the yarn in place around the needle with the thumb and index finger of your right hand, push the right needle down and toward the back through the center of the stitch on the left needle. The right needle will now be behind the left needle. (Illus. D & E)

5. Pull the remaining yarn off the left needle by pulling the right needle to the right so the newly formed stitch slides off the left needle onto the right needle. (Illus. F)

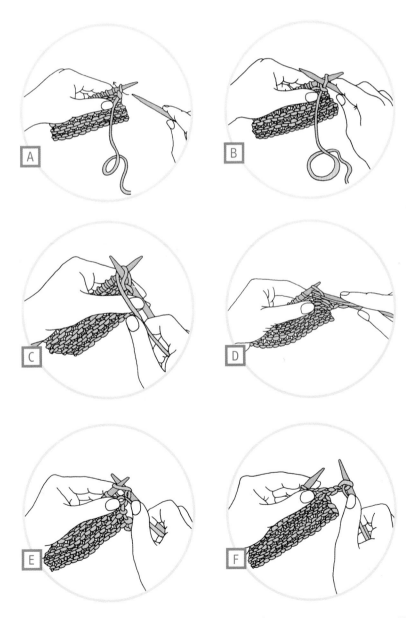

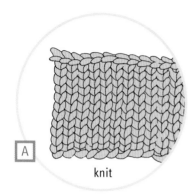

knit

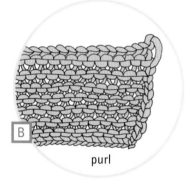

purl

Now you know how to knit and purl. If you alternate knitting a row and purling a row, you will be working in the most commonly used stitch, the stockinette stitch. This is universally abbreviated as **St st.** If you just knit or just purl on every row, then you are working in the garter stitch.

Stockinette can be achieved by the knit stitch alone when you knit in the round. Knitting in the round is exactly what it sounds like. Instead of knitting a row and transferring the stitches from one needle to another, you knit continuously in a circle. The most common uses for this are making hats and socks and adding roll-neck edges to sweaters.

To achieve a garter stitch when knitting in the round, you need to alternate knitting one round and purling one round.

So what would happen if you stopped working on your practice swatch and came back to it a few days later? Would you know what to do next? Look at both sides of the piece you have done so far. One side has stitches that resemble *V*s. (Illus. A) The other side should look like horizontal bars or maybe tiny pearls. (Illus. B) The *V*s are the knit stitches; the horizontal bars are the purls. So pick up your swatch. Place the empty needle in the right hand and the full needle in the left hand. Look at what is facing you. If the *V*s are facing you, then you are ready to do a knit row. If the horizontal bars are facing you, you are ready to do a purl row.

If you get interrupted in the middle of a row, it gets a bit trickier. Just remember that the needle with the ball of yarn attached should be in your right hand and the other needle in your left hand. Then look at the stitches and follow the rule above.

RIBBING

When you knit and purl stitches next to each other in the same row and then follow the pattern on the next row by knitting over your knit stitches and purling over your purls, you will create a ribbing. You can do a Knit 1, Purl 1 ribbing or a Knit 2, Purl 2 ribbing or any such variation. The key to making a ribbing is remembering that the yarn must be in *back* of your right needle when you are knitting and in *front* of your right needle when you are purling. In this book, we sometimes begin sweaters with a ribbing. It makes a nice border and prevents the edges from curling. You can also make a whole sweater with a rib pattern. The illustrations here show a Knit 2, Purl 2 ribbing.

to make a ribbing

1. Knit 2 stitches. (Illus. A)

2. Separate the needles slightly and bring the yarn from the back of your work to the front. Be sure you bring the yarn between the needles and not over a needle (which would cause you to add a stitch). (Illus. B)

3. Purl 2 stitches. (Illus. C)

4. After purling, you must bring the yarn between the needles to the back of the work before you knit 2 stitches again. (Illus. D)

5. Repeat these steps for your ribbing. Note how knit stitches (*V*s) are over knit stitches and purl stitches are over purl stitches. (Illus. E)

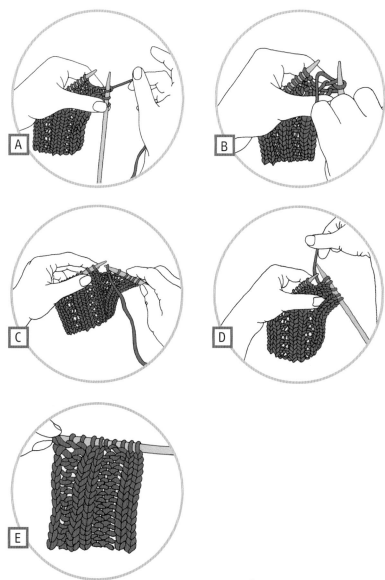

INCREASE AND DECREASE

Unless you are knitting a scarf, a blanket, or something else that is the same width from start to finish, you will need to add and subtract stitches during the course of your knitting project. The addition and subtraction of stitches is otherwise known as increasing and decreasing. While it is possible to increase and decrease on either the knit or the purl side of your work, there is rarely a need to do so while purling. The illustrations here show how to increase and decrease on the knit side.

INCREASING

Increasing is how you will add stitches to the number of stitches on a needle in order to add width to your knitted piece. The most common reason for increasing is shaping sleeves. A sleeve generally starts out narrow and get wider as it gets longer. This is accomplished by adding 1 stitch to each end of the needle every several rows.

You will encounter two methods for increasing in this book. The first is the bar method, known as Make 1, or **M1,** which is our preferred way to increase while knitting sleeves. Generally, we recommend you start a bar increase 2 stitches in from the edge of your work. This means you should knit 2 stitches, then do a bar increase, then knit until there are 2 stitches remaining on the left needle, then increase again. Increasing 2 stitches in from your edge makes sewing up the seam on your sleeve much easier because you can sew down a straight line that is uninterrupted by increases.

The second kind of increase is known as knitting into the front and back of a stitch. It is a quick and easy way to increase and is generally a good choice when you want your increases at the very edge of the knitted piece. We don't like this increase for sleeves because it tends to leave a slightly jagged edge that makes sewing more difficult; however, we used this method for The Princess's Poncho on page 134 because these edges don't get sewn up.

bar method
(also referred to as make 1, or m1)

1. At the point you wish to add a stitch, pull the needles slightly apart to reveal the bar located between 2 stitches. (see arrow, Illus. A)

2. With your left needle, pick up the bar from behind. (Illus. B)

3. Knit the loop you have made. Be sure to knit this loop as you would normally knit a stitch, going from the front of the stitch to the back. (Illus. C) Sometimes this stitch is a little tight and will be difficult to knit. In that case, gently push the loop up with your left forefinger, loosening the stitch and making it easier to insert your right needle.

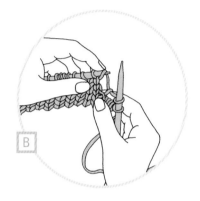

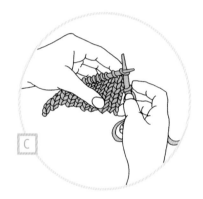

knitting into the front and back of a stitch

1. Begin to knit into the stitch you are going to increase into. Stop when you have brought the right needle through the stitch on the left needle and it is forming the *X* in the front. (Illus. A) DO NOT take the stitch off the left needle as you normally would when completing a knit stitch.

2. Instead, leave the stitch on the left needle and move the tip of the right needle so it is behind the left needle. (Illus. B)

3. Insert the right needle into the back of the stitch on the left needle (Illus. C) and knit it again—wrap yarn around the back needle counterclockwise. Hold the yarn against the needle with your right hand and guide the needle toward you through the center of the stitch. The right needle should end up on top of the left needle.

4. Pull the stitch off the left needle. You now have 2 stitches on the right needle. (Illus. D)

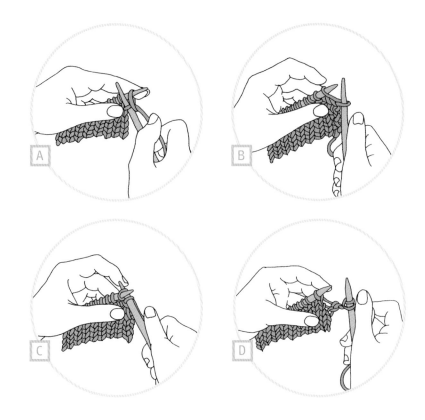

DECREASING

Decreasing is how you will reduce the number of stitches on a needle in order to narrow the width of your knitted piece. The most common use for decreases is shaping armholes and necks.

In this book, we use two methods of decreasing. The first is a slip, slip, knit, abbreviated as **SSK.** This is a left-slanting decrease. The other method is a Knit 2 together, abbreviated as **K2tog.** This is a right-slanting decrease.

slip, slip, knit (ssk)

We use this method when we want our decreases to slant toward the *left*.

1. One at a time, slip 2 stitches as though you were going to knit them (Knitwise), to the right needle. (Slipping a stitch means that you insert your right needle into the loop on the left needle as though you were going to knit it BUT you don't complete the knit stitch; you just slide the stitch off the left needle onto the right needle.) (Illus. A)

2. Insert the left needle into the front of the 2 slipped stitches, forming an *X*, with the left needle in front of the right needle. (Illus. B)

3. Wrap the yarn counterclockwise around the back needle and knit the 2 slipped stitches together, slipping the completed new stitch onto the right needle. (Illus. C & D)

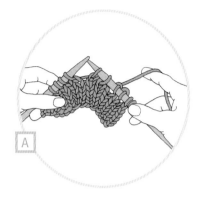

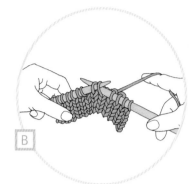

knit 2 together (k2tog)

We use this technique when we want our decreases to slant to the *right*.

1. Working on a knit row, insert your right needle from front to back into the second and then the first stitch you want to knit together. (Illus. A)

2. Bring the yarn around the needle and complete the stitch as though you were knitting a regular stitch. (Illus. B & C)

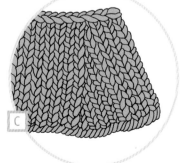

BIND OFF

Binding off is how you get your knitted piece off the needles and prevent it from unraveling. You bind off when you are finished with your blanket, when you are shaping a neck or armholes, or when you have completed the front or back of a sweater. We will explain what shaping a neck and shaping an armhole mean later on; for now, all you need to learn is how to bind off. You can bind off on a knit or a purl row. The concept is the same either way. We illustrate how to bind off on a knit row.

1. Knit 2 stitches. (Illus. A)

2. Insert the left needle into the front of the first stitch on the right needle. Using the left needle, pull the first stitch up and over the second stitch. (Illus. B) You can place your forefinger on the second stitch to hold it in place and keep it from coming off the needle.

3. Now push that stitch off the left needle completely. (Illus. C & D)

4. Knit one more stitch and repeat the last two steps. Continue this process until you have bound off the desired number of stitches.

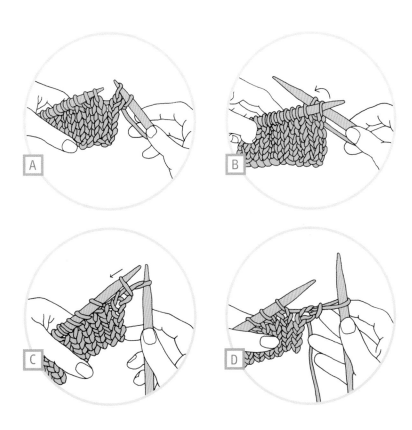

When you are binding off all your stitches at the end of a blanket or when you are done knitting a section of your sweater, you should have 1 loop left on the right needle. At this point, cut the yarn, leaving 3 or 4 inches, and pull the end through the remaining loop to tie it off.

YARN OVERS

A yarn over (abbreviated **YO**) basically allows you to make a hole in your knitting on purpose—as opposed to those inadvertent holes made by dropping stitches. Yarn overs are generally used for lace knitting or to make a buttonhole.

yarn over before a knit

If the stitch after the yarn over will be a knit, use this method of making a yarn over:

1. Hold both needles with the fingers of your left hand and hold the yarn with your right hand in back of the right needle. (Illus. A)

2. Pull the yarn up and around the right-hand needle from the front to the back. (Illus. B) You created the yarn over, which is just a loop.

yarn over before a purl

If the stitch after the yarn over will be a purl, use this method:

1. Hold both needles with the fingers of your left hand and hold the yarn with your right hand in front of the right needle. (Illus. A)

2. Pull the yarn up and around the needle counterclockwise, from the front to the back and to the front again. (Illus. B)

COLOR WORK

We use two types of color work in our patterns. Striping is the easiest way to incorporate different colored yarns into a knitted project. You can stripe with as many colors as you want. Once your colors are attached (just as simple as starting a new ball of yarn), all you need to do is drop the color you are working with and pick up the color you need to use next. You begin and end a stripe at the beginning of a row. Intarsia is a technique used to add or change color in the middle of a row. You will need to use bobbins (holders for a small amount of yarn) for most intarsia projects. For this book, we used only two colors at a time so you don't need to use bobbins; you can use the whole balls of yarn.

striping

1. Work the number of desired rows in color A. Leave the yarn of color A attached. (Illus. A)

2. Add in color B by looping the new yarn around the right needle (Illus. B) and knitting the first stitch.

3. Work the number of desired rows in color B.

4. To switch back to color A, let go of color B and pick up color A. (Illus. C & D)

5. Knit with color A for the number of desired rows. (Illus. E)

6. Continue striping until the required length. (Illus. F)

If you are making very wide stripes, you might prefer to cut the yarn each time you switch colors. Otherwise, just leave the unused yarn hanging until it is time to alternate colors.

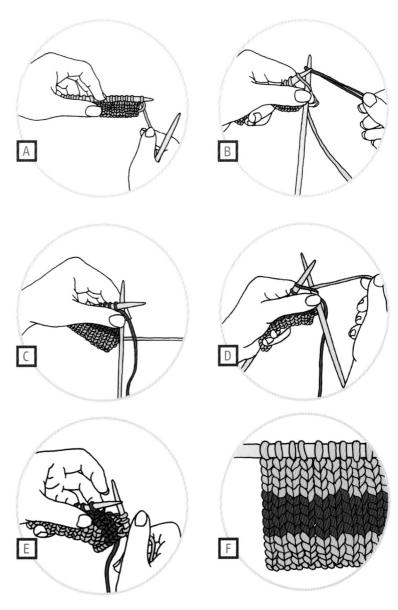

intarsia

1. Cast on the desired number of stitches with color A and color B. (Illus. A)

2. Knit across the stitches of color B, then pick up color A and bring it under color B. (Illus. B)

3. Begin knitting the stitches in color A. (Illus. C)

4. Purl across the stitches of color A. (Illus. D)

5. Pick up color B and bring it under color A and then begin purling the stitches in color B. (Illus. E)

6. This is what the knit side of your work should look like. (Illus. F)

7. This is what the purl side of your work should look like. (Illus. G)

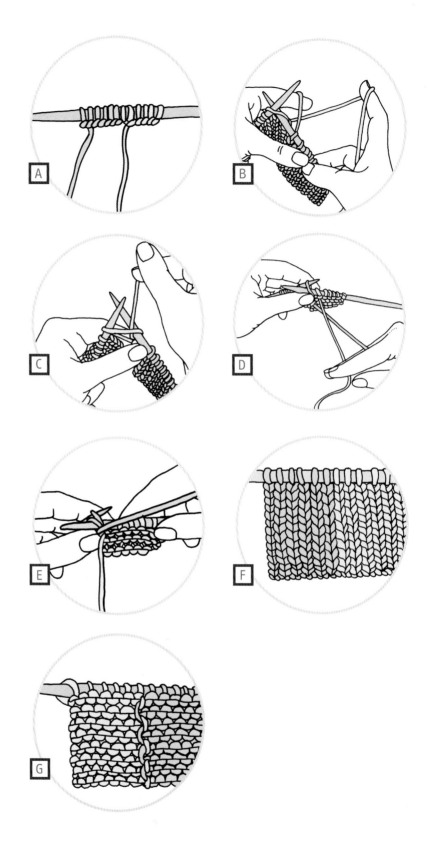

BOBBLE

Bobbles are little raised bumps that provide a nice textural detail to anything you are knitting. We think they are really cute when added to the bottom of a sweater, although you can place them anywhere.

1. Begin to knit the stitch you are going to make the bobble out of. Stop when you have brought the right needle through the stitch on the left needle and it is forming the X in the front. DO NOT take the stitch off the left needle as you normally would when completing the knit stitch. (Illus. A)

2. Leave the stitch on the left needle and move the tip of the right needle so it is behind the left needle. (Illus. B)

3. Insert the right needle into the back of the stitch on the left needle and knit it again. (Illus. C)

4. Now you have made 2 stitches out of 1. Do not take the loop off the left-hand needle. Instead, bring the right needle to the front and knit the loop on the left needle. Continue until you have knit into the front, back, front, back, front of the stitch. (Illus. D)

5. You will have 5 stitches on the right needle. (Illus. E)

6. Turn your work so the needle with the five stitches is in the left hand. (Illus. F) Knit these five stitches. Turn your work and purl these five stitches. Turn again, knit these five, and then turn and purl these five once more. Turn and knit 2 together, k1, knit 2 together, turn and P3 together.

You have completed your bobble. (Illus. G)

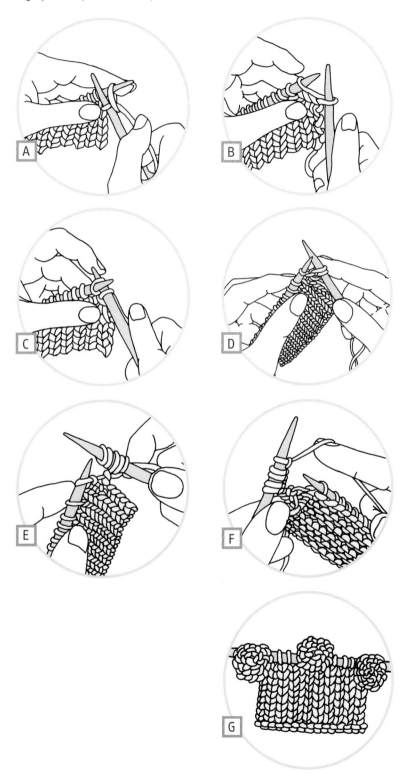

CAST ON IN THE MIDDLE OF ROW

You will need to cast on in the middle of a row when your project requires a hole in the middle of a row. We designed a hole in the bunting (see page 152) so a car seat or stroller straps can pass through it. Before you cast on in the middle of a row, you need to bind off those stitches on the row before. This is done exactly as you would when shaping the neck for a crew-neck pullover. This technique is also an alternative way to make buttonholes.

1. Work to where the cast-off stitches are. (Illus. A)

2. Turn work so the yarn is attached to the stitches on the left needle. (Illus. B)

3. Insert the right needle into the first stitch on the left needle and knit it, but do not take it off the left needle. (Illus. C)

4. Bring the left needle to the front and right of the stitch on the right needle and then insert the left needle into the stitch on the right needle. (Illus. D)

5. Transfer the stitch from the right to the left needle. (Illus. E)

6. You have now cast on 1 stitch in the middle of the row.

7. Repeat these steps until you have cast on the desired number of stitches in the middle of the row.

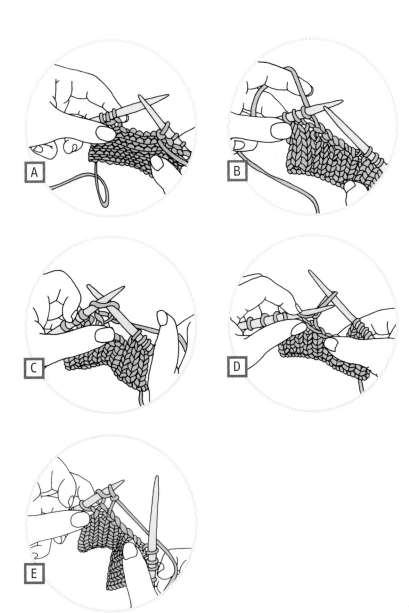

FINISHING TECHNIQUES

You can spend hours knitting row after row of perfect ribbing and flawless stockinette stitch, but all those efforts can be undermined by sloppy finishing technique. Knowing how to sew a sweater together properly is the key to whether the sweater looks handmade—or homemade. Finishing a sweater is the bane of many a knitter's existence, but it doesn't have to be. If you use the proper techniques, the process should be relatively painless and your sweater should look virtually seamless. And a final steaming, known as blocking, will smooth over any inconsistencies or bumpy seams.

Some tips:

◉ This may go against every instinct you possess, but sweaters are always sewn on the right side. This means that unlike regular sewing, where the two right sides of your garment are facing each other when you sew, in knitting **the right sides face out.**

◉ Although other people might tell you differently, we prefer **not** to use the yarn we knit our sweater with to sew it together. If your garment is sewn together properly, you will not see any of the yarn used for sewing on the right side. This means, theoretically, that you should be able to sew your black sweater together with hot pink yarn. Generally, we suggest using a needlepoint yarn in a similar color because using a different yarn allows you to see what you are doing much more clearly. And, dare we say it, it also enables you to rip out what you have done, if necessary, without inadvertently damaging the sweater itself.

Whether you are making a V-neck, turtleneck, crew neck, or cardigan, sweaters are always assembled in the same order:

1. Sew shoulder seams together.

2. Sew sleeves onto sweater.

3. Sew sleeve seams from armhole to cuff.

4. Sew side seams from armhole to waist.

Once the pieces are joined together, you can add crochet edgings, pick up stitches for a neck, create button bands for a cardigan, or embellish with other finishing touches.

sewing shoulder seams

1. Lay the front and back of your sweater flat with the right sides facing you and the shoulders pointing toward each other. If you are sewing the shoulder seams of a cardigan together, make sure the neck and armholes are facing in the correct direction, with the armholes facing away from the center and the neck toward the center. (Illus. A)

2. Cut a piece of sewing yarn approximately twice the width of your shoulder seam and thread it through a darning needle.

3. Secure the sewing yarn to the garment by making a knot with one end of the sewing yarn on the inside shoulder edge of the back of your sweater.

4. Insert the needle into the first stitch at the shoulder edge of the front of the sweater. Your needle should have passed under 2 bars and should be on the right side or outside of the work. (Illus. B)

5. Now place the needle under the corresponding stitch of the back of your sweater. (Illus. C) Next, insert the needle into the hole the yarn is coming from on the front and go under the next stitch. Then do the same thing on the back. This is how you continue to weave the sweater together. It is easier if you keep the yarn relatively loose because it is easier to see the hole your yarn is coming from. Pull the sewing yarn tight after you have 6 or 7 stitches and just loosen the last stitch before you proceed.

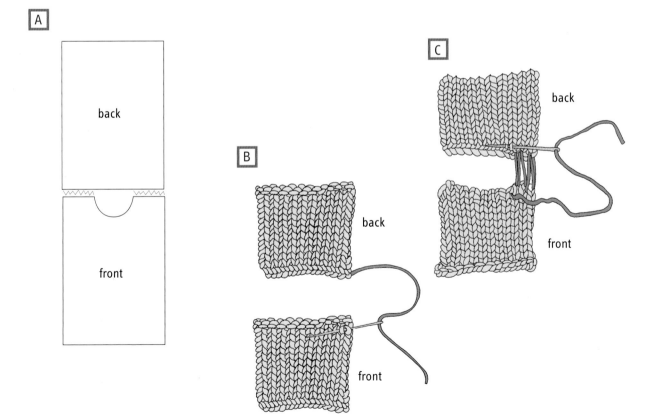

sewing the sleeves to the body

IMPORTANT: WHEN YOU SEW SLEEVES ONTO THE BODY, MAKE SURE THEY COME DOWN TO THE CORRECT PLACE.

This aspect of finishing is relatively painless because the sweaters in this book are all drop sleeve. This means there are no armholes. So you need to determine how many inches you need on either side to evenly sew the sleeve from the shoulder seam down the side. Before you start sewing, just place a marker at these points and adjust your sewing as you go along. You do not want the sleeve to be too narrow or too wide. You have knit the sleeve to a certain width at the top and it should, if sewn in properly, hit the right spot, but you do need to make sure.

These measurements are a guide to help you find the right spot.

0–3 months: 5″ • 3–6 months: 5.5″ • 1 year: 6″ • 2 years: 6.5″ • 3 years: 7″

1. Cut a piece of yarn approximately 20″ long and thread it through a darning needle.

2. Attach the yarn to the body of the sweater by poking the needle through the edge of the shoulder seam you made when sewing the shoulders together. Pull the yarn halfway through and make a knot. You should now have half the yarn going down one side of the armhole and half going down the other side.

3. Find the center of the upper sleeve edge by folding the sleeve in half. With the yarn needle, pull the yarn under the center 2 bars on the sleeve. (Illus. A) Your sleeve is now attached to the body of the sweater.

4. Now you need to find 2 bars on the body of the sweater. Start at the top near the shoulder seam. This is slightly different from finding the bars on the sleeves because the bars on the sleeves are stitches and on the body, the bars will be rows. Place the needle 1 full stitch in on the body of the sweater and find the 2 bars. (Illus. B)

5. Continue sewing as for the shoulders, taking 2 bars from the body and 2 bars from the sleeve and pulling the yarn every few stitches until the sewing yarn is no longer visible and until the sleeve is sewn into the armhole. (Illus. C & D)

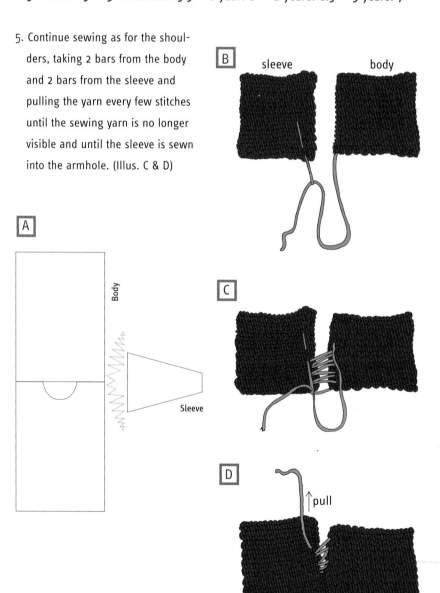

sewing side & sleeve seams

1. Cut a piece of yarn approximately twice the length of the sleeve and side seam.

2. Attach the yarn by inserting the sewing needle through the two seams at the underarm. Pull the yarn halfway through and make a knot. Half of the yarn should be used to sew the side seam and half should be used to sew the sleeve seam.

3. It doesn't matter whether you start with the body or the sleeve. For both, find the 2 vertical bars 1 full stitch in from the edge and begin the sewing process (Illus. A), taking 2 bars from one side of the sweater and then 2 bars from the other side. (Illus. B) Make sure you are going into the hole where the yarn last came out and pulling the yarn every few stitches. (Illus. C)

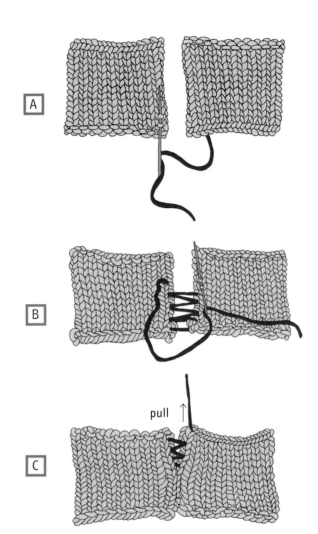

sewing up rolled edges

When sewing up a project that has rolled edges, you will want to finish it off so you don't see the seam when the fabric rolls. The way you do this is to sew your seam as you always do, on the right side of the work, BUT at about 1 inch or so before you reach the bottom, you must start sewing on the wrong side of the work instead of the right side. The seam will then show up on the right side, but the roll edge will cover it.

picking up stitches

Once the pieces of your sweater are joined, you need to make a nice finished edge for the neckline. If you are making a cardigan, you will also need to add button bands on each side, one with buttonholes and the other a solid strip to which you will attach the buttons. Rather than knit these elements as separate pieces that are then sewn on, we like to knit them directly onto the finished sweater. In order to do this, you must pick up stitches along the finished edges. When you pick up the stitches for a neck, you are generally picking up stitches horizontally in an already-made stitch. When picking up for button bands, you pick up the stitches vertically, in rows. Either way, the method for picking up the stitches is the same; the difference is where you place the needle to pick up the next stitch. You can pick up stitches in existing stitches (vertically Illus. A–E) or in rows (horizontally Illus. F–J).

1. Place the work with the right side facing you. Starting at the right edge of your piece with the knitting needle in your right hand, place the needle in the first stitch, poking through from the outside to the inside. (Illus. A & B; F & G)

2. Loop the yarn under and around the needle and pull the needle back through that same stitch. There should be 1 stitch on the needle. (Illus. C & D; H & I)

3. Continue to poke the needle through each stitch, wrapping the yarn around the needle as if you were knitting and adding a stitch to the needle each time. (Illus. E & J).

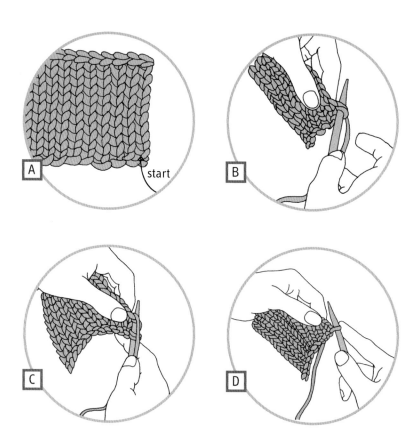

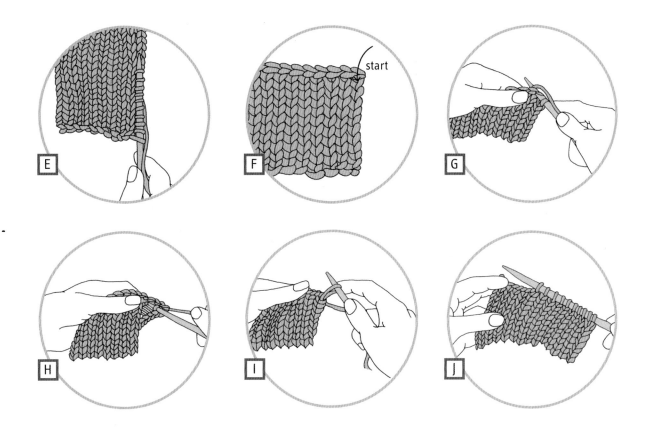

When you are picking up stitches in stitches, as for a crew-neck pullover, most of the time you want to pick up every stitch. It is important to note that there is an extra hole between each stitch. So picking up every stitch is the same thing as picking up every other hole. If you poke your needle through every consecutive hole, you will pick up too many stitches.

When you are picking up stitches in rows, as when you are picking up button bands, you do not want to pick up a stitch in *every* row. To determine how often to pick up, note your gauge. If your gauge is 3 stitches to the inch, then you will want to pick up stitches in 3 consecutive rows, then skip 1 row and repeat this process. If your gauge is 4 stitches to the inch, you will want to pick up stitches in 4 consecutive rows and then skip 1 row. It is necessary to skip a row every so often because there are more rows per inch than stitches per inch. If you were to pick up a stitch in every row, when you started to knit these picked-up stitches, you would have too many stitches and the button bands would look wavy.

weaving in ends

Beginner knitters are often baffled by what to do with all the loose ends. Don't worry about them until you sew your projects together. While you are knitting, try to keep your ends about 4 inches long. Remember this when you are adding a new ball of yarn or casting on or binding off. If the ends are long enough, you can weave them in with a sewing needle. All you do is thread the needle with an end and weave the yarn back and forth through the seam 3 to 4 times. Then snip the end. You do not need to make a knot. If the ends are too short, you can use a crochet hook, but this is a bit harder.

blocking

Sometimes when a garment is completely assembled, it requires a bit of shaping. Blocking allows you to reshape the piece gently by applying steam, which relaxes the yarn fibers so they can be stretched in order to smooth out bulky seams, even out uneven knitting, or even enlarge a too-small garment.

Not every piece needs to be blocked; use your common sense. But if you do decide some reshaping or smoothing is in order, pin your garment onto a padded ironing board, easing it into the desired shape. If your iron can emit a strong stream of steam, hold the iron above the piece without touching it and saturate it with steam. Otherwise, dampen a towel, place it over the garment, and press with a warm iron. Allow the piece to remain pinned to the ironing board until it is completely cool.

Never apply a hot iron directly to a knitted piece, and always read the label on your yarn before blocking; some fibers should not be blocked.

FINISHING TOUCHES

Fringe, I-cords, pom-poms, and tassels are nice finishing touches for hats, scarves, blankets, and ponchos. Before you begin, you will need a few things. For fringe, you will need a piece of cardboard, a crochet hook, a pair of scissors, and yarn. For an I-cord, you need a circular or double-pointed needle and yarn. For pom-poms, you need a pom-pom-maker, which you can buy from your yarn store (or you can try to make your own using cardboard), a crochet hook, scissors, and yarn. For tassels, you need a piece of cardboard, scissors, and yarn.

fringe

A very popular finishing touch for blankets and ponchos, fringe is commonly used to accent scarves.

To make the fringe, cut a piece of cardboard as tall as the length of fringe you desire. Then wrap the yarn around the cardboard approximately 20 times. (If you need more fringe than this, you can repeat the step.) Then cut the strands of yarn across the top of the cardboard. You now have strands of yarn that are twice your desired length. If you want thick fringe, use several strands of yarn; if you want thinner fringe, use only a strand or two.

VERY IMPORTANT:

TO FILL IN THE FRINGE ON A PIECE OF WORK, WE SUGGEST YOU START BY ATTACHING FRINGE AT EACH EDGE AND THEN AT EACH MIDWAY POINT UNTIL YOU ARE SATISFIED.

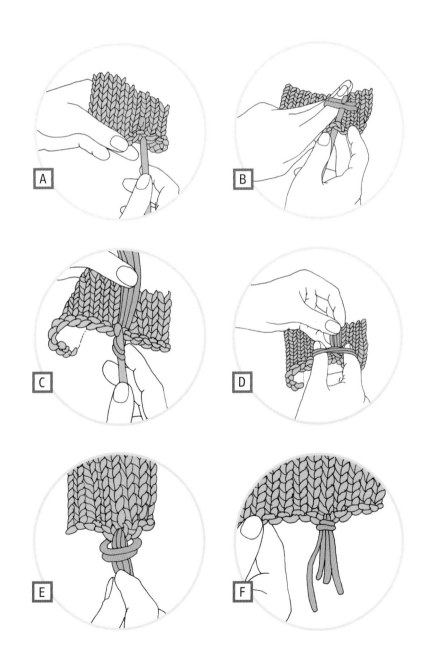

1. To attach fringe to your knitted garment, insert your crochet hook through a stitch at one of the ends of your knitted piece. You should take the crochet hook from underneath the piece to the top of it, and the crochet hook should be facing you. (Illus. A)

2. Fold your strands of yarn in half and grab the center of these strands with your hook. Pull these strands through the stitch. (Illus. B & C)

3. Remove the crochet hook and place your fingers through the loop you made with the strands of yarn. Then pull the loose ends through this loop. (Illus. D & E)

4. You have completed one fringe. (Illus. F) Cut the ends to even them if you prefer.

i-cords

You can add I-cords, which are basically knitted ropes, to the top of a hat to add a little pizzazz. I-cords are also great for purse handles and as cords in a sweatshirt.

1. Using a double-pointed or circular needle, cast on and knit 3 stitches. (Illus. A)

2. Slide these stitches toward the right to the other end of the needle. (Illus. B)

3. Place the needle in your left hand. The yarn will be attached to the stitch farthest to the left. (Illus. C)

4. Pick the yarn up from behind and knit the 3 stitches. (Illus. D & E)

5. Repeat steps 2–4 until your I-cord reaches the desired length.

6. This is what your I-cord should look like. (Illus. F)

7. To end the I-cord, K3tog and pull the yarn through the remaining loop to fasten.

pom-poms

We made two pom-poms for our Jester Hat (page 124). You can also add them to the bottom of a poncho or the corners of a blanket.

1. Wrap yarn around the pom-pom-maker tightly, so there is no space between strands of yarn. (Illus. A) You can use your fingers or a crochet hook to pull yarn through the center of the pom-pom-maker.

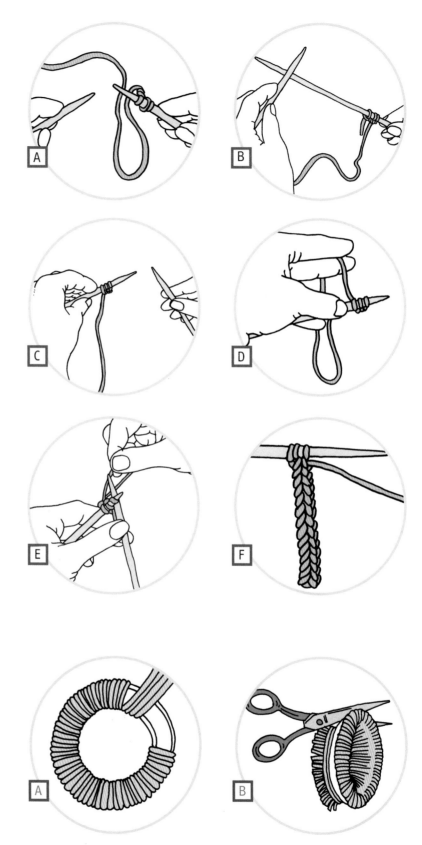

2. Cut these strands in the groove of the pom-pom-maker. (Illus. B)

3. Place a piece of yarn inside this groove and tie it tightly. (Illus. C) Remove the pom-pom-maker.

4. A completed pom-pom should look like this. (Illus. D)

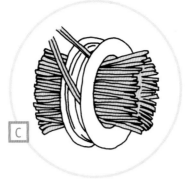

tassels

Tassels are another fun option when adding details to hats. They also look great on the ends of a blanket or a poncho.

1. Cut a piece of cardboard a little longer than you want your tassel to be. Wind yarn around the cardboard tightly and compactly to desired thickness. (Illus. A)

2. Place a strand of yarn under the strands on the cardboard so each loose strand of yarn is on either side. (Illus. B)

3. Tie the strand closed at the top. (Illus. C)

4. Cut the strands of yarn on the bottom end of the cardboard (Illus. D) and remove the cardboard.

5. Tie a strand of yarn around the bundle about 1 inch from the top of the tassel. (Illus. E)

6. Pull this yarn through the center of the top of the tassel and attach to your knitted garment. (Illus. F)

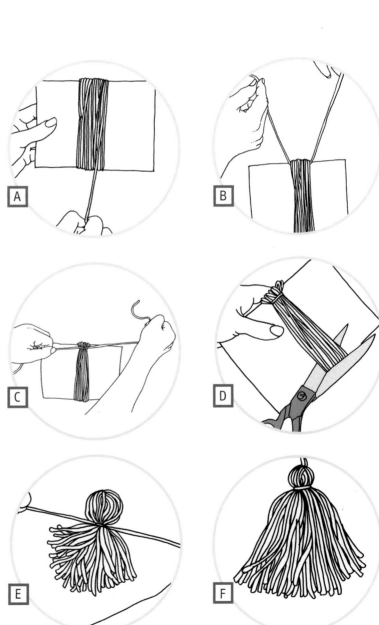

SINGLE CROCHET AND SHRIMP STITCH

Even if you have never crocheted—and never plan to—it's useful to know a couple of basic crochet techniques for finishing off a knitted piece. Using a crochet stitch for edgings gives sweaters and throws a nice, polished look. Shrimp stitch gives a sturdy corded look. Generally, you want to use a crochet hook that matches the size knitting needle you used. For instance, if you used a size 6 knitting needle, you should use a size 6 (also known as size G) crochet hook.

single crochet

1. With the right side of the work facing you, insert your crochet hook through a stitch under the bind-off. (Illus. A)

2. Grab the yarn with the crochet hook and pull it through the stitch to the front of your work. (Illus. B) You will now have 1 loop on the crochet hook. (Illus. C)

3. Insert the crochet hook through the next stitch, hook the yarn, and pull it through the stitch. You now have 2 loops on the crochet hook. (Illus. D & E)

4. Hook the yarn and pull it through both of the loops on the crochet hook. (Illus. F) You will end up with 1 loop on the hook. Insert the hook through the next stitch and repeat across the entire row, ending with 1 loop on the hook.

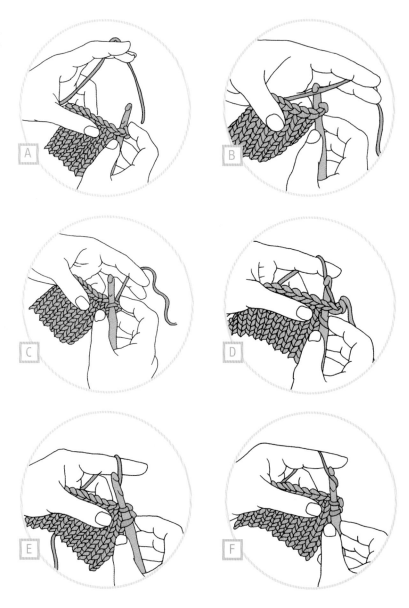

shrimp stitch

This is also known as backwards crochet because you work from left to right instead of right to left. You must do 1 row of single crochet (abbreviated **SC**) before you begin the shrimp stitch.

1. Make a slip stitch by grabbing the yarn through the loop on the hook. (Illus. A)

2. Keeping your right index finger on the loop, insert the hook into the next stitch to the right from the right side to the wrong side of the work. (Illus. B & C)

3. Grab the yarn with the hook and pull it through to the right side of the work. (Illus. D)

4. You should have 2 loops on the hook. (Illus. E)

5. Grab the yarn with the hook and pull it through the 2 loops. (Illus. F & G)

6. Repeat in the next stitch to the right. (Illus. H)

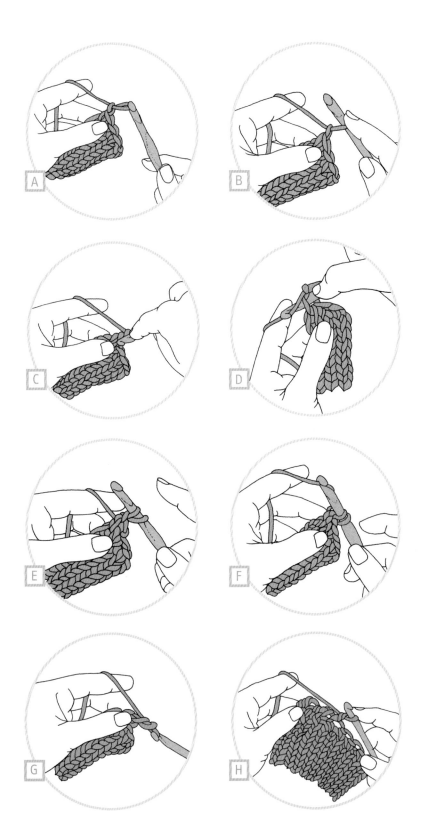

gauge page

THE MOST IMPORTANT MESSAGE IN THIS CHAPTER IS THAT
YOU MUST ALWAYS MAKE A GAUGE SWATCH!
IF YOU DON'T MAKE A GAUGE SWATCH, THERE ARE NO
GUARANTEES THAT YOUR SWEATER WILL FIT PROPERLY!

You just spent time and money picking out yarn to make the perfect baby sweater. You're eager to get to work and most of all, you can't wait to see how cuddly the baby will look in his adorable new togs. In order for this scenario to have a happy ending, it is crucial that you understand gauge. A grasp of gauge will save you the misery of having to rip out your knitting because your hoped-for size small looks like it could fit Baby Huey. And it will help you avoid the depression that comes from investing hours of time on an unwearable garment. If you're not yet a master of gauge, read this information carefully!

STITCH GAUGE = THE NUMBER OF STITCHES REQUIRED TO PRODUCE 1 INCH OF KNITTED FABRIC

Gauge is the most important—and most misunderstood—element of knitting. Simply put, stitch gauge determines the finished measurements of your garment. Technically—and yes, it is a technical, even mathematical concept—stitch gauge tells you the number of stitches you'll need to knit to produce a piece of knitted fabric 1 inch wide.

For each pattern in this book you will find the garment's finished measurements. If your gauge is off, the finished knitted piece will not have the proper dimensions for the size you have chosen. It is, therefore, important to refer to these finished measurements as you knit, making certain your gauge has not changed and that the finished piece will have the correct measurements.

A pattern is always written with a specific gauge in mind, and if you do not get the gauge just right, your project won't turn out as the pattern designer intended.

Here's a simple example: If a pattern says your stitch gauge should be 3 stitches to the inch, that means 60 stitches should produce a piece of knitted fabric 20 inches wide. This is because 60 stitches divided by 3 (your gauge) equals 20 inches. If your gauge were 4 stitches to the inch, you would need to cast on 80 stitches to produce the same 20-inch width.

It really is just that easy: simple division and multiplication, and you can even use a calculator—we do!

All patterns state the stitch gauge (or tension, if it's not an American pattern) required to achieve the desired measurements for your finished garment. The gauge swatch is always knit in the same stitch you'll use for the garment itself. Usually a pattern will tell you that your stitch gauge should be measured over 4 inches (or 10 centimeters if, again, it's not American). For example, under "gauge" your pattern may say "16 stitches = 4 inches." This means that your stitch gauge should be 4 stitches to the inch. Patterns also generally include a row gauge, which indicates how many rows you need to knit in order to get a piece of knitted fabric 1 inch long. For most of the patterns in this book, row gauge is not particularly important, so you really only have to worry about stitch gauge.

Along with the gauge, patterns also recommend a needle size to get a particular stitch gauge with a particular yarn. DO NOT assume that just because you are using a pattern's suggested yarn and needle size you don't have to do a gauge swatch. Everybody knits differently. Some people are loose knitters, some are tight

knitters, and some are in the middle. Whatever type of knitter you are, you can always get the required gauge eventually, but you may need to make some adjustments. Tight knitters will have to go up in needle size, while loose knitters will have to use needles a size smaller. Remember, it's far more important to get the specified gauge than to use the specified needle—or yarn, for that matter.

Here's how to check your gauge:

Cast on 4 times the number of stitches required per inch. For example, if the gauge is 4 stitches = 1 inch, cast on 16 stitches; if your gauge is supposed to be 3 stitches = 1 inch, cast on 12 stitches.

Work in the pattern stitch using the needle size recommended for the body of the sweater. Sometimes ribbing is knit on smaller needles, but you shouldn't use the smaller size for your gauge.

When your swatch is approximately 4 inches long, slip it off the needle and place it on a flat surface. Measure the width of your swatch. If it measures 4 inches wide, you're getting the required gauge and can begin your knitting project.

If your swatch is more than 4 inches wide, your knitting is too loose. Reknit your swatch on needles a size or two smaller and measure again. Repeat as necessary, using smaller needles until you get the correct gauge.

If your swatch is less than 4 inches wide, you are knitting too tight. Reknit your swatch on needles a size or two larger and measure the swatch again. Repeat as necessary, using larger needles until you get the correct gauge.

You should also know that gauge can change as you make your garment. This happens for a multitude of reasons and does not mean you are a bad knitter. Please check the width of what you are knitting once the piece measures about 3 inches long. Compare it to the measurements the pattern provides and make adjustments in the needle size if necessary.

REMEMBER:
Always knit a gauge
swatch—*Always!!*

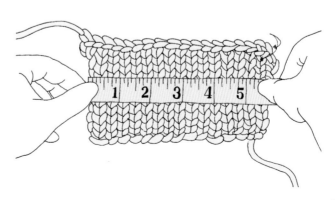

HELPFUL HINTS

We know you want to get to the good stuff—the patterns—but if you read over these helpful hints and keep them in mind as you knit, you might save yourself from ripping out rows of stitches or untangling a gaggle of knots.

using multiple strands of yarn

In some patterns, we used more than one strand of yarn. This means we knit with two or more strands of yarn as though they were one. We did this because we really liked a certain yarn, but it wasn't thick enough as a single strand. To use multiple strands of yarn, you can wind the separate balls into one ball. We find this easier than working from two or more balls at once. You do not need to hold the yarn any differently. Work as though there is one strand. Do not worry if the strands twist.

attaching new yarn when shaping the neck for a pullover

When you have finished binding off for one side of a neck on a V-neck or crew-neck pullover, you will be instructed to attach the yarn and continue binding off on the other side of the neck. Make sure you attach the yarn in the center of the sweater and not at the outside or shoulder edge.

increasing on sleeves

You can begin to increase on sleeves on the row after the ribbing. If there is a rolled edge, you can begin after 4 rows. When the instructions tell you to increase every 4th row, this means after the first time you increase. You do not need to work 4 rows after the ribbing and then begin to increase.

This is where your increasing should occur on a stockinette sweater where you are increasing every 4th row:

Row 1: Knit-Increase

Row 2: Purl

Row 3: Knit

Row 4: Purl

Repeat rows 1–4 until the required number of increases have been worked.

striping: to cut or carry

When you are striping, you should try to carry your yarn. This means you should not cut the yarn each time you need to use a new color. You will have two or more balls of yarn hanging. If you are using more than two colors, we suggest placing the balls in plastic baggies when you are not using them. The reason to carry the yarn is that sewing the sweater together will be much easier and neater if you do. You will not have tons of ends to weave in. However, there are a few instances where you might want to cut the yarn. The first is if you do not need to use a color again for many inches. The other is if all the balls hanging are driving you mad.

choosing yarn for baby's sweater

For many knitters, the second most exciting part of a project (after getting big compliments from the parents!) is picking out the yarn. There are so many delicious new yarns on the market today, in lush colors and irresistible textures, you may feel like a kid in a candy store when you shop for yarn. We do, and we own the candy store!

We have noted the specific yarn we used for each pattern as well as the number of balls we used and the yardage. However, if you can't find the same yarn for any reason—it could be discontinued, or your shop just might not carry it—you can easily substitute yarns, as long as you choose a yarn or combination of yarns that gets the same gauge as the yarn we used.

Also, just because we used double strands of yarn doesn't necessarily mean you must. If you prefer to substitute a yarn that knits to the required gauge using a single strand, that's okay. Just be sure that when you choose a different yarn, you base the amount you will need on the yardage and not on the number of grams or balls. For example, if we use 5 balls of yarn that have 100 yards in each ball and we are knitting with a single strand of yarn, we are using 500 yards of yarn. If the yarn you like has 50 yards per ball, you will need 10 balls. Or, if we use 8 balls of a yarn that has 100 yards and we are using a double strand of yarn, we are using 800 yards. But if you want to use a yarn that gets the same gauge with a single strand and it has 80 yards per ball, you will need only 5 balls.

A FEW LAST THINGS
BEFORE YOU BEGIN

The following are terms you may encounter in the knitting patterns in this book. Read through this section before you start a project so when you encounter a reference to reverse shaping or see an asterisk in your knitting directions, it won't throw you for a loop.

knitting markers

When you need to mark off a designated number of stitches on your needle—say, to mark the center of a V-neck—you may be instructed to place a marker on the needle. You can buy markers at your yarn shop or just make your own by tying a short strand of yarn in a color that contrasts with your piece into a loop.

needle size

Needles come in sizes from less than 0 all the way up to 50. Your needle size helps determine your gauge (see the Gauge Page), and you need to use different size needles with different yarn weights and thicknesses. A size 0 needle has a very small diameter and is used with very, very fine yarns to make tightly textured, fine work, especially for baby clothes. A size 7 needle is a medium-size needle that is generally used with medium-weight yarn. A size 50 needle looks like a turkey baster and is used with incredibly chunky yarn or many strands knitted together at once. This produces a very thick knitted fabric.

reverse shaping

We use this term when we want you to make two pieces, one the mirror image of the other. When you shape the neck on a pullover, you bind off the center stitches and then finish one side of the sweater at a time. On one side you will have to shape the neckline in one direction (while knitting) and on the other side you will have to shape it in the other direction (while purling). Also, when you make a cardigan, you make two front sections—one that will be the right side when worn and one that will be the left side when worn—and must shape the necklines and armholes in opposite directions. The easiest way to visualize this is to shape one side without really thinking about it and then, when you get to the neck shaping on the second side, lay both pieces out as they would be on the finished sweater. You will see what the second neckline needs to look like.

yardage

Yardage helps you determine how many balls of yarn you will need for your project. Many books and patterns tell you that you need a certain number of grams or ounces, but in our experience this is an inaccurate way to determine the amount of yarn you will need, as different fibers have different weights. Acrylic is a much lighter fiber than wool: A 50-gram ball of acrylic yarn might contain 200 yards, whereas a 50-gram ball of wool might contain only 125 yards. Therefore, if a pattern called for 200 grams of acrylic yarn and you bought 200 grams of wool instead, you would be 300 yards short. In this book, we always specify the total number of yards needed for each pattern.

knitting glossary

BIND OFF (CAST OFF)

This is the way you get stitches off the needle at the end of a project. Cast off is also a method used to decrease stitches.

CAST ON

This is how you put stitches onto your needle to begin a project.

DEC.

Decrease. This is how you take stitches away once you have begun knitting. We use two methods of decreasing in this book, SSK and K2tog.

EDGE STITCH

An edge stitch is exactly what it sounds like: the stitch at the edge of your work. Some of our patterns call for an edge stitch, and this means that we want you to knit the first and last stitch on every row, no matter what the rest of the pattern requires.

GARTER STITCH

Knit every row. But if you are knitting in the round (on a circular needle), then garter stitch means you should knit 1 round and purl the next.

INC.

Increase. This is how you add a stitch onto your needle once you have begun knitting. We use two methods of increasing in this book, a bar increase (Make 1, abbreviated **M1**) and knitting into the front and back of a stitch.

K

Knit.

K2TOG

Knit 2 stitches together. This is a method of decreasing. It slants your decrease toward the right.

P

Purl.

REV ST ST

Reverse Stockinette Stitch. P1 row, K1 row, and the purl side is the right side of the garment.

RS

Right side. This is the side that will face out when you are wearing the garment. In this book, the RS is always the knit side.

SC

Single crochet.

SEED STITCH

Seed stitch is like a messed-up ribbing. As for ribbing, you alternate knitting and purling, but instead of knitting on the knit stitches and purling on the purl stitches to create ribs, you purl over your knit stitches and knit over your purl stitches to create little "seeds."

SSK

Slip, Slip, Knit. This is a method of decreasing. It slants your decrease toward the left.

ST ST

Stockinette Stitch. Knit 1 row, purl 1 row. But if you are knitting in the round (on a circular needle), then St st means you should knit every round.

WS

Wrong Side. This is the side that will face in when you are wearing the garment. In St st, the WS is always the purl side.

YARN DOUBLED

When you knit with the yarn doubled, you are working with 2 strands of yarn held together as though they were 1. Yarn tripled means working with 3 strands of yarn held together. It is no harder to knit with 2 or 3 strands of yarn than it is to knit with 1. When we tell you to use a yarn doubled or tripled, it means the yarn we used for the pattern needed to be thicker than it actually is in order to achieve the proper gauge. If you prefer not to double or triple yarn, try substituting a bulkier yarn that knits to the gauge with a single strand. Just remember that if you use a single strand of yarn where we used 2, you will need only half the yardage to complete the pattern, or one third if the yarn is tripled.

YO YARN OVER.

This is how you make a hole in your work (on purpose).

★ . . . . . ★

In knitting patterns, asterisks are used to indicate that a series of stitches is to be repeated. Repeat only what is between the asterisks, not what is outside of them. For example, **K2, *(K2, P2)*** 3 times means K2, K2, P2, K2, P2, K2, P2. ***(K5, K2tog)* across row** means that you should K5, K2tog, K5, K2tog, and so on across the whole row.

the yarn girls' favorite kid Patterns

Now it's time for the patterns. Over the years, these sweaters, hats, and blankets have proven to be our favorites as well as our customers' favorites. This book has patterns for newborns to kids three years of age. However, you will notice that when we used yarn thicker than 4 stitches to the inch, the smallest size is for a one-year-old. The projects (except for the dresses, the ponchos, and the bunting) are all knit in two color ways in order to show that almost any pattern is appropriate for a girl or a boy if you just use the right colors. Of course, you don't have to stick to our color choices. Feel free to be creative and pick your own colors—that is half the fun of knitting! But in case you need some help in this area, we show additional color possibilities for certain projects. Finally, we have Basic and Beyond Basic chapters. The Basic chapters include the simplest options. The Beyond Basic chapters introduce simple stitch and color work.

For each of the patterns that follow we provide the general information that tells you what type of yarn to use, the fiber content, and how much of it you need. We also tell you the finished measurements for each size. We then provide directions for knitting the sweater. Directly after the patterns are step-by-step guides that focus on the trickier aspects of making the projects. The step-by-steps are there to help you with such things as shaping the armhole, crew neck, or V-neck, and in some cases increasing in pattern on the sleeves. If you follow these instructions to the letter, you should be able to master the procedure even if you are a novice who has never done any shaping or increasing in pattern before. At the same time, you will be creating an adorable and wearable piece of knitted clothing for a little one.

The beauty of these patterns is their versatility. Once you're comfortable with a given pattern and have mastered its more challenging elements, you can get a little creative. Try mixing and matching different edgings or necks, or make the crewneck sweater you love as a turtleneck. You can also try out new stitches and apply them to a basic project shape. Just remember, you still must get the correct gauge in your pattern stitch.

We want your knitting to go as smoothly as possible, so please read the tips that follow *before* you knit. It beats having to come back later searching for a clue to what went wrong after you've put in several hours on your project.

> Once you're comfortable with a given pattern and have mastered its more challenging elements, you can get a little creative.

some words of wisdom

MAKE SURE YOU HAVE *ALL* THE MATERIALS REQUIRED BEFORE YOU START YOUR PROJECT. Knitting patterns are like recipes in that everything you need to make the finished product is listed at the beginning. Your pattern should tell you the required stitch gauge, the recommended needle size, the type of yarn used, the number of balls needed, the yardage per ball, and the finished measurements of the garment.

MAKE SURE YOU KNIT A GAUGE SWATCH TO GUARANTEE YOU ARE GETTING THE REQUIRED STITCH GAUGE. (Obviously, we can't stress this enough.) Also, in order to get a good fit, you should always know the finished measurements of your garment. Knitting patterns always state these, either on a diagram or written out. You should measure the width of the piece you are knitting every few inches to ensure you will in fact produce a piece of knitted fabric that conforms to the specified measurements of the project you are making. Even if you got the gauge when you knit your gauge swatch, check the measurements along the way. Sometimes people knit their actual garments tighter or looser than they did their swatch. This happens to the best of us, so always remeasure and make adjustments if necessary. If your measurement is *not* correct, you *must* rip out the knitting you have done (if you've been measuring all along, it will be only a few inches) and start over. Go down a needle size or two if the garment is too big and up a needle size or two if it is too small.

BEFORE YOU START KNITTING, READ OVER YOUR PATTERN. Make sure the actual knitting instructions make sense to you. See if you understand all the abbreviations and techniques. If you are confused by anything, you have several options:

REMEMBER THAT YOUR KNITTING BOOK IS YOUR BEST RESOURCE. In this book and most other knitting books is a glossary that defines and explains the various techniques and abbreviations used (see page 00). If you don't remember what WS stands for, you can turn to the glossary, which will tell you that WS means wrong side. It will also explain what wrong side means. If you are confused by something more complex, such as how to do an SSK, refer to the diagram in the how-to section.

 YOU CAN CROSS-REFERENCE. If you find the definitions in a given book unclear, check out another book. Knitting books often explain things slightly differently, and one book might provide an explanation that is easier for you to understand than another. Also, remember that people learn things in different ways. Some are very visual, and looking at a diagram is all they need in order to figure something out. Others do better by reading written instructions, and yet others need someone to actually show them how things are done. If you are one of the latter, don't hesitate to march back down to the store from which you purchased your yarn to get a few pointers.

 SOMETIMES THINGS JUST DON'T MAKE SENSE UNTIL YOU ACTUALLY DO THEM. You can always knit your project up to the point where things start to get bewildering, then read the pattern carefully and work *exactly* as instructed—even if you can't quite visualize the outcome. You'll be surprised how often things make sense after you've done a row or two.

 DON'T FREAK OUT WHEN YOU FINISH A BALL OF YARN. It is easy to add a new ball. Just tie the ends of the old and new balls together with a double knot, leaving strands on both that are long enough to weave in. Try to attach the new ball at the end of a row, not in the middle. If you can't, you can't—but if you aren't sure the yarn you have left will make it across the row, be safe and start a new ball.

Common sense is perhaps the most important thing to rely on when knitting a pattern. Don't blindly follow a pattern your gut tells you is wrong. That is a recipe for disaster. Always look at what you are doing and ask yourself if it looks correct. Does it look too big or too small? Is it lopsided? Don't you need armholes on *both* sides of your sweater? Simple common sense may help you avoid pitfalls. Don't be afraid to trust your instincts.

> Don't blindly follow a pattern that your gut tells you is wrong. That is a recipe for disaster.

basic pullovers

Pullover sweaters for babies are great beginner projects. They are easy to knit, yet they introduce various basic techniques throughout the project. We like to begin knitting a sweater with the back piece. We do this for two reasons. First, the back of a sweater is a simple square (or sometimes a rectangle)—so it is no more difficult than a scarf. There is no neck shaping, no armhole shaping, and no shoulder shaping because we make our baby sweaters with drop sleeves. Second, we like to start with the back because sometimes things don't always go perfectly at the beginning of a project. A stitch might look funny, and tension may be a little erratic. If this occurs, it is a little easier to shrug your shoulders and say, "That's OK, it's the back. It's not smack dab in the front of my sweater." Knitting the back piece first allows you to work through any kinks before it really matters.

After the back is done and you've got the hang of things, it's time to knit the front. The front piece is almost the same as the back, except a few inches before you reach the top of the sweater you shape the neck. This isn't difficult—it's just new. You need to bind off stitches in the center of a row and continue shaping the neck one side at a time. Then when you knit the sleeves, you learn how to increase. And once you have all the pieces completed, sewing up the seams and picking up stitches are the final techniques to master.

The three pullovers in this chapter introduce you to these techniques. *Lickety-Split Knit* is a chunky roll-neck sweater. It is about as easy as a sweater can get. To achieve a rolled edge, all you do is simple stockinette stitch the whole way up—no ribbing. *Julie's Itchy Fingers* is a basic crew-neck sweater with a knit 2, purl 2 ribbing around the edges. Because this sweater is knit with a slightly smaller-gauge yarn than the others, we included sizing for newborns. *Master of Her Own Domain* is a little different than the other two sweaters because it has a funnel neck rather than a crew neck. This requires neither neck shaping nor picking up stitches. Plus, this sweater is knit in garter stitch. All you have to do is knit, knit, knit . . . it's as easy as that.

lickety-split knit

Deborah used to make lots of sweaters for her nephew Sammy on little needles, using baby-weight yarn. She had invested hours upon hours on each sweater only to find that Sammy grew out of these beautiful creations in less time than it had taken to make them. Fed up with this predicament, she asked us what she could do. She still wanted to make beautiful sweaters for Sammy but didn't want to spend so much time doing it. We suggested a chunky knit sweater. Deborah hesitated because she thought a chunky sweater might be too cumbersome for little Sammy, but we assured her that one-year-olds could definitely wear it, and wear it comfortably. Deborah said, "What the heck, I'll try it," and she made this sweater in a weekend. She gave it to Sammy the following week, and it looked great. Even though Sammy outgrew it in a few months, Deborah didn't feel bad because she knew she could whip up another in no time.

BACK:

With #15 needle, cast on 24 (28, 30) stitches. Work in St st until piece measures 13" (14½", 16") from cast-on edge, ending with a WS row. Bind off all stitches loosely.

FRONT:

Work as for back until piece measures 10½" (12", 13½") from cast-on edge, ending with a WS row. **Shape Crew Neck:** Bind off center 6 stitches and then begin working each side of the neck separately. At the beginning of each neck edge, every other row, bind off 2 stitches 1 time, 1 stitch 2 times. (See step-by-step instructions.) Continue to work on remaining 5 (7, 8) stitches with no further decreasing until piece measures 13" (14½", 16") from cast-on edge, ending with a WS row. Bind off all stitches loosely.

SLEEVES:

With #15 needle, cast on 14 (14, 16) stitches. Work in St st. **AT THE SAME TIME,** increase 1 stitch at each edge every 4th row 5 (7, 7) times until you have 24 (28, 30) stitches.

NOTE: INCREASE LEAVING 2 EDGE STITCHES ON EITHER SIDE OF WORK. THIS MEANS YOU SHOULD KNIT 2 STITCHES, INCREASE 1 STITCH, KNIT TO THE LAST 2 STITCHES, INCREASE 1 STITCH, AND THEN KNIT THE REMAINING 2 STITCHES. INCREASING LIKE THIS MAKES IT EASIER TO SEW UP YOUR SEAMS.

Continue in St st until sleeve measures 7½" (8½", 10½") from cast-on edge, ending with a WS row. Bind off all stitches loosely.

FINISHING:

Sew shoulder seams together. Sew sleeves to body. Then sew up side and sleeve seams. With a 16" circular #15 needle, pick up 30 (32, 32) stitches around the neck. Work in St st (all knit) in rounds for 4 rows. Bind off all stitches loosely.

lickety-split knit, for her

YARN: LANG LA PAZ (38 YARDS / 50G BALL)

FIBER CONTENT: 72% MERINO WOOL / 28% POLYAMIDE

COLORS:
GIRL VERSION: #97
BOY VERSION: #35

AMOUNT: 5 (6, 8) BALLS

TOTAL YARDAGE: 190 (228, 304) YARDS

GAUGE: 2 STITCHES = 1 INCH; 8 STITCHES = 4 INCHES

NEEDLE SIZE: US #15 (10MM) FOR BODY OR SIZE NEEDED TO OBTAIN GAUGE; 160 CIRCULAR US #15 (10MM) FOR PICKING UP STITCHES AROUND NECK

SIZES: 1 YEAR (2 YEAR, 3 YEAR)

KNITTED MEASUREMENTS: WIDTH = 12" (14", 15"), LENGTH = 13" (14½", 16"), SLEEVE LENGTH = 7½" (8½", 10½")

STEP-BY-STEP GUIDE TO SHAPING THE CREW NECK

Remember that after binding off the center stitches, you will work one side at a time.

ROW 1: Knit 11 (13, 14) stitches; with the 10th (12th, 13th) stitch, begin to bind off the center 6 stitches. For example, for the 1-year size, this means you should pull the 10th stitch over the 11th stitch, and this is your first bind-off. When you are done binding off the center 6 stitches, check to make sure you have 9 (11, 12) stitches on each side of the hole, including the stitch on the right-hand needle. Knit to end of row. Turn work.

ROW 2: Purl. Turn work.

ROW 3: Bind off first 2 stitches. Knit to end of row. Turn work.

ROW 4: Purl. Turn work.

ROW 5: Bind off 1 stitch. Knit to end of row. Turn work.

ROW 6: Purl. Turn work.

ROW 7: Bind off 1 stitch. Knit to end of row. Turn work.

ROW 8: Purl. Turn work.

• For the other side of the neck edge, attach yarn to the remaining stitches and begin binding off 2 stitches immediately. You will now be binding off when you are purling. Finish neck shaping as for the other side and bind off.

• When you are done with the bind-off instructions, compare the length of the front piece to the length of the back. If the front and back measure the same, bind off the remaining stitches. If the front is too short, continue knitting and purling until the pieces are of equal length, then bind off.

During Julie's pregnancy, she had itchy fingers to knit for her daughter-to-be. But between running The Yarn Company, writing this book, knitting projects for this book, and being pregnant, she was exhausted. She needed a project that would not require any concentration but would still look special. She chose this sweater-and-hat

julie's itchy fingers

combo because of its simple pattern. After a long day, she could come home and sit on the couch to relax and knit. To give the sweater and hat a special feel, she chose a fun yarn with a unique texture and a pleasing color palette. Now she just has to wait for her baby to grow into the sweater.

hat

With #9 needle, cast on 56 (60, 62, 64, 68) stitches. Work in St st stitch for 4 rows. Change to #7 needle and work in K2, P2 ribbing for 4 rows as follows: For 1-year size: Row 1: K2 *(P2, K2)* to end. Row 2: P2 *(K2, P2)*. Repeat rows 1 and 2. For 0–3 months, 3–6 months, 2-year, and 3-year sizes: K2, P2 for 4 rows. Change to #9 needle and work in St st until piece measures 5" (5½", 5¾", 6", 6") from cast-on edge ending with a WS row. Work decreases as follows:

ROW 1: *(K5 stitches, K2tog)* to end of row.

ROWS 2, 4, 6, 8, AND 10: Purl.

ROW 3: *(K4 stitches, K2tog)* to end of row.

ROW 5: *(K3 stitches, K2tog)* to end of row.

ROW 7: *(K2 stitches, K2tog)* to end of row.

ROW 9: *(K1 stitch, K2tog)* to end of row.

ROW 11: *K2tog* to end of row.

Cut yarn, leaving approximately 20". With a yarn needle, thread yarn through remaining loops and sew down seam. Make a pom-pom and attach to the top of the hat.

sweater

BACK:

With #7 needle, cast on 40 (44, 48, 52, 60) stitches. Work in K2, P2 ribbing for 4 rows. Change to #9 needle and work in St st until piece measures 10" (11", 12", 13½", 15") from cast-on edge, ending with a WS row. Bind off all stitches loosely.

FRONT:

Work as for back until piece measures 8" (9", 9½", 11", 12½") from cast-on edge, ending with a WS row. **Shape Crew Neck:** Bind off center 12 (12, 12, 14, 14) stitches and then begin working each side of the neck separately. At the beginning of each neck edge, every other row, bind off 3 stitches 1 time, 2 stitches 1 time, 1 stitch 2 times. (See step-by-step instructions.)

Continue to work on 7 (9, 11, 12, 16) remaining stitches with no further decreasing until piece measures 10" (11", 12", 13½", 15") from cast-on edge, ending with a WS row. Bind off all stitches loosely.

SLEEVES:

With #7 needle, cast on 26 (26, 28, 30, 32) stitches. Work in K2, P2 ribbing for 4 rows as follows: For 0–3 months, 3–6 months, and 2-year sizes: Row 1: K2 *(P2, K2)* to end. Row 2: P2 *(K2, P2)*. Repeat rows 1 and 2. For 1-year and 3-year sizes: K2, P2 for 4 rows. Change to #9 needles. Work in St st. **AT THE SAME TIME,** increase 1 stitch at each edge every 4th row 7 (8, 9, 11, 11) times until you have 40 (42, 46, 52, 54) stitches.

YARN: PRISM, COTTON CREPE (75 YARDS / 50G BALL)

FIBER CONTENT: 100% COTTON

COLORS:
GIRL VERSION: CANTINA
BOY VERSION: SAHARA

AMOUNT: 4 (4, 5, 6, 7) BALLS

TOTAL YARDAGE: 300 (300, 375, 450, 525) YARDS

GAUGE: 4 STITCHES = 1 INCH; 16 STITCHES = 4 INCHES

NEEDLE SIZE: US #9 (5.5MM) FOR BODY OR SIZE NEEDED TO OBTAIN GAUGE; US #7 (4.5MM) FOR RIBBING; 16" CIRCULAR US #7 (4.5MM) FOR PICKING UP STITCHES AROUND NECK

SIZES: 0–3 MONTHS (3–6 MONTHS, 1 YEAR, 2 YEAR, 3 YEAR)

KNITTED MEASUREMENTS: SWEATER: WIDTH = 10" (11", 12", 13", 15"), LENGTH =10" (11", 12", 13½", 15"), SLEEVE LENGTH = 6" (6½", 7", 8", 10") HAT CIRCUMFERENCE: 14" (14¾", 15½", 16", 17")

NOTE: INCREASE LEAVING 2 EDGE STITCHES ON EITHER SIDE OF WORK. THIS MEANS YOU SHOULD KNIT 2 STITCHES, INCREASE 1 STITCH, KNIT TO THE LAST 2 STITCHES, INCREASE 1 STITCH, AND THEN KNIT THE REMAINING 2 STITCHES. INCREASING LIKE THIS MAKES IT EASIER TO SEW UP YOUR SEAMS.

Continue in St st until sleeve measures 6" (6½", 7", 8", 10") from cast-on edge, ending with a WS row. Bind off all stitches loosely.

FINISHING:

Sew shoulder seams together. Sew sleeves on to body. Then sew up side and sleeve seams. With a circular 16" #7 needle, pick up 60 (60, 60, 64, 64) stitches around the neck. Work in K2, P2 ribbing for 4 rows, then work in St st for 4 rows. Bind off all stitches loosely.

STEP-BY-STEP GUIDE TO SHAPING THE CREW NECK

Remember that after binding off the center stitches, you will work one side at a time.

ROW 1: Knit 16 (18, 20, 21, 25) stitches; with the 15th (17th, 19th, 20th, 24th) stitch begin to bind off the center 12 (12, 12, 14, 14) stitches. For example, for the 0–3 month size, you should pull the 15th stitch over the 16th stitch, and this is your first bind-off. When you are done binding off the center 12 (12, 12, 14, 14) stitches, check to make sure you have 14 (16, 18, 19, 23) stitches on each side of the hole, including the stitch on the right-hand needle. Knit to end of row. Turn work.

ROW 2: Purl. Turn work.

ROW 3: Bind off first 3 stitches. Knit to end of row. Turn work.

ROW 4: Purl. Turn work.

ROW 5: Bind off first 2 stitches. Knit to end of row. Turn work.

ROW 6: Purl. Turn work.

ROW 7: Bind off 1 stitch. Knit to end of row. Turn work.

ROW 8: Purl. Turn work.

ROW 9: Bind off 1 stitch. Knit to end of row. Turn work.

ROW 10: Purl. Turn work.

• For the other side of the neck edge, attach yarn to the remaining stitches and begin binding off 3 stitches immediately. You will now be binding off when you are purling. Finish neck shaping as for the other side and bind off.

• When you are done with the bind-off instructions, compare the length of the front piece to the length of the back. If the front and back measure the same, bind off the remaining stitches. If the front is too short, continue knitting and purling until the pieces are of equal length, then bind off.

julie's itchy fingers, for her

master of her own domain

People learn at their own pace, and we know some students need a little more time than others to master knitting techniques. Amanda, who took our beginner class, was one of those students. She took the class at the suggestion of a friend who picked up knitting and purling in a jiffy and by the end of class left with the materials to begin a sweater. Amanda intended to leave class with the same project. However, she could only master the knit stitch during the class. There is really no rhyme to our reason, but most of the sweater patterns we write are for stockinette or some more slightly complicated stitch, and not garter. But, as Amanda was determined to make a baby sweater, we wrote this pattern for her. She finished her sweater in no time and was then ready to conquer purling. Amanda was thrilled, and we got to add a new sweater to our repertoire.

master of her own

domain, for her

YARN: SCHAEFER YARNS, ELAINE (300 YARDS / 225G BALL)

FIBER CONTENT: 99% MERINO WOOL / 1% NYLON

COLOR:
GIRL VERSION: MISS POPPINS
BOY VERSION: MR. GREEN JEANS

AMOUNT: 1 (2, 2) BALL(S)

TOTAL YARDAGE: 300 (600, 600) YARDS

GAUGE: 3 STITCHES = 1 INCH; 12 STITCHES = 4 INCHES

NEEDLE SIZE: US #11 (8MM) OR SIZE NEEDED TO OBTAIN GAUGE

SIZES: 1 YEAR (2 YEAR, 3 YEAR)

KNITTED MEASUREMENTS: WIDTH= 12″ (13$\frac{1}{3}$″, 15$\frac{1}{3}$″), LENGTH =12″ (13$\frac{1}{2}$″, 15″), SLEEVE LENGTH = 7″ (8″, 10″)

BACK AND FRONT (make 2):

With #11 needle, cast on 36 (40, 46) stitches. Work in garter stitch until piece measures 12″ (13$\frac{1}{2}$″, 15″) from cast-on edge. **Shape Funnel Neck:** Bind off 8 (10, 12) stitches at the beginning of the next 2 rows. (See step-by-step instructions.) Continue to work in garter stitch on remaining 20 (20, 22) stitches for 8 more rows. Bind off all stitches loosely.

SLEEVES:

With #11 needle, cast on 18 (22, 24) stitches. Work in garter stitch. **AT THE SAME TIME,** increase 1 stitch at each end every 4th row 7 (8, 9) times, until you have 32 (38, 42) stitches.

NOTE: INCREASE LEAVING 2 EDGE STITCHES ON EITHER SIDE OF WORK. THIS MEANS YOU SHOULD KNIT 2 STITCHES, INCREASE 1 STITCH, KNIT TO THE LAST 2 STITCHES, INCREASE 1 STITCH, AND THEN KNIT THE REMAINING 2 STITCHES. INCREASING LIKE THIS MAKES IT EASIER TO SEW UP YOUR SEAMS.

Continue in garter stitch until sleeve measures 7″ (8″, 10″) from cast-on edge. Bind off all stitches loosely.

FINISHING:

Sew shoulder seams and neck together. Sew sleeves to body. Then sew up side and sleeve seams.

STEP-BY-STEP GUIDE TO SHAPING THE FUNNEL NECK

ROW 1: Bind off 8 (10, 12) stitches, knit to end. Turn work.

ROW 2: Bind off 8 (10, 12) stitches, knit to end. Turn work.

ROW 3: Knit to end of row. Turn work.

Repeat row 3 7 more times.

Bind off all stitches loosely.

beyond basic pullovers

The three pullovers included in this chapter take the knitter one step beyond the simple stockinette or garter stitch sweater. Each pattern adds a little something extra so the beginner knitter can learn a new technique while quickly finishing a relatively simple project.

Like Father, Like Sons has a four-quadrant design. Merely knitting half of the stitches and purling the other half create this design. *This Is It!* is based on an uncomplicated two-row pattern that yields an intricate-looking rib pattern. Everyone is sure to be impressed if you knit this sweater, yet you need not let on that it was really simple. *This Is It!* also requires the knitter to learn how to increase in pattern, which can sometimes get a little tricky, but if you are up for a little bit of a challenge, it's a great thing to learn. And don't worry, we explain exactly how to increase in pattern in the step-by-step guide.

Even Daniele Did It, Again is essentially a straightforward stockinette stitch sweater, but it brings the use of different colors into the mix. Working with color can sometimes be a complicated proposition, but stripes couldn't be easier. Stripes require little extra effort, yet they allow you to play with color and to create a sweater with a bit more interest than one that is solid-colored.

like father, like sons

Each year for Christmas, Deb makes matching sweaters for her two boys, Quentin and Teddy. Knowing how insanely busy it gets before the holidays, she wanted to make sweaters that looked great but that she could knit up quickly and painlessly. She remembered a pattern she'd knit for her husband several years ago and asked if we could size it down for her boys. Of course we could! So after a few quick calculations to adjust the pattern, she chose this great bulky yarn, and now she has a wonderful picture of her husband and her two boys posing in front of the Christmas tree in their matching sweaters. And we have this terrific four-quadrant pattern that looks great for mothers and daughters, too!

BACK:

With #17 needle, cast on 24 (28, 30) stitches. Work 6 rows in St st. Then work 12 (14, 15) stitches in knit and 12 (14, 15) stitches in purl. Continue in this knit 12 (14, 15), purl 12 (14, 15) pattern until piece measures 7½″ (8″, 9″) from cast-on edge. Then work 12 (14, 15) stitches in purl and 12 (14, 15) stitches in knit. Continue in this purl 12 (14, 15) knit 12 (14, 15) pattern until piece measures 12½″ (14″, 15½″) from the cast-on edge, ending with a WS row. Bind off all stitches loosely.

FRONT:

Work as for back until piece measures 10″ (11½″, 13″).

NOTE: DON'T FORGET TO PURL 12 (14, 15), KNIT 12 (14, 15) AT 7½″ (80, 90)

Shape Crew Neck: Bind off center 6 (8, 8) stitches and then begin working each side of the neck separately. At the beginning of each neck edge, every other row, bind off 2 stitches 1 time and 1 stitch 1 time. (See step-by-step instructions.) Continue to work on remaining 6 (7, 8) stitches with no further decreasing until piece measures 12½″ (14″, 15½″) from cast-on edge, ending with a WS row. Bind off all stitches loosely.

YARN: ZITON, VARIO (33 YARDS / 50G BALL)

FIBER CONTENT: 100% WOOL

COLORS:
GIRL VERSION: 60
BOY VERSION: 70

AMOUNT: 6 (7, 8) BALLS

TOTAL YARDAGE: 198 (231, 264) YARDS

GAUGE: 2 STITCHES = 1 INCH; 8 STITCHES = 4 INCHES

NEEDLE SIZE: US #17 (12MM) OR SIZE NEEDED TO OBTAIN GAUGE; 16″ CIRCULAR US #15 (10MM) FOR PICKING UP STITCHES AROUND THE NECK.

SIZES: 1 YEAR (2 YEAR, 3 YEAR)

KNITTED MEASUREMENTS: WIDTH = 12″ (14″, 15″), LENGTH = 12½″ (14″, 15½″), SLEEVE LENGTH = 7″ (8″, 10″)

like father, like sons.
for him

SLEEVES:

With #17 needle, cast on 14 (16, 16) stitches. Work in St st for 6 rows. Then work 7 (8, 8) stitches in knit and 7 (8, 8) stitches in purl. Continue in this pattern until piece measures 4″ (5″, 6″). Then reverse and work the first set of stitches in purl and the others in knit. **AT THE SAME TIME,** increase 1 stitch at each end every 4th row 4 (5, 6) times until you have 22 (26, 28) stitches. When increasing on these sleeves, the pattern changes slightly. For example, for the 1-year size, you start by knitting 7 stitches and purling 7 stitches. After the first increase, you will be knitting 8 stitches and purling 8 stitches. After the second increase, you will be knitting 10 stitches and purling 10 stitches. When sleeve measures 7″ (8″, 10″) from cast-on edge ending with a WS row, bind off all stitches loosely.

NOTE: INCREASE LEAVING 2 EDGE STITCHES ON EITHER SIDE OF WORK. THIS MEANS YOU SHOULD WORK 2 STITCHES, INCREASE 1 STITCH, WORK TO THE LAST 2 STITCHES, INCREASE 1 STITCH, AND THEN WORK THE REMAINING 2 STITCHES. INCREASING LIKE THIS MAKES IT EASIER TO SEW UP YOUR SEAMS.

FINISHING:

Sew shoulder seams together. Sew sleeves on and then sew up side and sleeve seams. With a circular 16″ #15 needle, pick up 32 (36, 36) stitches around the neck and work in St st for 6 rows. Bind off all stitches loosely. (Remember that St st is all knit when you are working in the round.)

STEP-BY-STEP GUIDE TO SHAPING THE CREW NECK

Remember that after binding off the center stitches, you will work one side at a time.

ROW 1: Purl 11 (12, 13) stitches; with the 10th (11th, 12th) stitch begin to bind off the center 6 (8, 8) stitches. For example, for the 1-year size this means you should pull the 10th stitch over the 11th stitch, and this is your first bind-off. When you are done binding off the center 6 stitches, check to make sure you have 9 (10, 11) stitches on each side of the hole, including the stitch on the right-hand needle. Knit to end of row. Turn work.

ROW 2: Purl. Turn work.

ROW 3: Bind off 2 stitches. Knit to end of row. Turn work.

ROW 4: Purl. Turn work.

ROW 5: Bind off 1 stitch. Knit to end of row. Turn work.

ROW 6: Purl. Turn work.

• For the other side of the neck edge, attach yarn to the remaining stitches and begin binding off 2 stitches immediately. You will still be binding off on a knit row. Finish neck shaping as on other side and bind off remaining stitches.

• When you are done with the bind-off instructions, compare the length of the front piece to the length of the back. If the front and back measure the same, bind off the remaining stitches. If the front is too short, continue knitting and purling until the pieces are of equal length, then bind off.

this is it!

When Edith found out her granddaughter, Maya, was pregnant, she was delighted to find a great-grandchild was on the way. Edith couldn't wait to begin knitting, and she wanted to make something special for this bundle of joy. However, she didn't want to take on a project with complicated stitches, little needles, or too many colors. Edith saw this sweater hanging up on our wall and said, "This is it! This is the sweater! The rib pattern is simple, the needles are nice and big, and the color is in the yarn!"

BACK:

With #11 needle, cast on 37 (39, 45) stitches. Work in garter/rib pattern as follows:

For 1-year size: Row 1: P2 *(K3, P3)* across row, end K3, P2. Row 2: Purl. For 2-year and 3-year sizes: Row 1: K3 *(P3, K3)* to end. Row 2: Purl. Repeat rows 1 and 2 until piece measures 12″ (13½″, 15″) from cast-on edge, ending with a row 2. Bind off all stitches loosely.

FRONT:

Work as for back in garter/rib pattern until piece measures 9½″ (11″, 12½″) from cast-on edge, ending with a row 2. **Shape Crew Neck:** Bind off center 9 (11, 11) stitches and then begin working each side of neck separately. At the beginning of each neck edge, every other row, bind off 3 stitches 1 time, 1 stitch 2 times. (See step-by-step instructions.) Continue to work in pattern on remaining 9 (9, 12) stitches until piece measures 12″ (13½″, 15″) from cast-on edge, ending with a row 2. Bind off all stitches loosely.

SLEEVES:

With #11 needle, cast on 22 (22, 25) stitches. Work in garter/rib pattern as follows: For 1-year and 2-year sizes: Row 1: K2, *(K3, P3)* to last 2 stitches, K2. Row 2: Purl. For 3-year size: Row 1: K2, *(K3, P3)* to last 5 stitches K3, K2. Row 2: Purl. Continue in the garter/rib pattern. **AT THE SAME TIME,** increase 1 stitch at each edge every 4th row 7 (8, 9) times until you have 36 (38, 43) stitches. (See step-by-step instructions.)

NOTE: INCREASE LEAVING 2 EDGE STITCHES ON EITHER SIDE OF WORK. THIS MEANS YOU SHOULD KNIT 2 STITCHES, INCREASE 1 STITCH, WORK IN GARTER/RIB PATTERN TO THE LAST 2 STITCHES, INCREASE 1 STITCH, AND THEN KNIT THE REMAINING 2 STITCHES. INCREASING LIKE THIS MAKES IT EASIER TO SEW UP YOUR SEAMS. ALSO ON THIS PATTERN YOU SHOULD WORK YOUR INCREASES INTO THE GARTER/RIB PATTERN.

Continue to work in garter/rib pattern until sleeve measures 7″ (8″, 10″) from cast-on edge, ending with a row 2. Bind off all stitches loosely.

YARN: CRYSTAL PALACE YARNS, ICELAND (109 YARDS / 100G BALL)

FIBER CONTENT: 100% WOOL

COLORS:
GIRL VERSION: 7243
BOY VERSION: 7251

AMOUNT: 3 (4, 4) BALLS

TOTAL YARDAGE: 327 (436, 436) YARDS

GAUGE: 3 STITCHES = 1 INCH; 12 STITCHES = 4 INCHES (IN PATTERN STITCH)

NEEDLE SIZE: US #11 (8MM) OR SIZE NEEDED TO OBTAIN GAUGE; CIRCULAR 16″ US #11 (8MM) FOR PICKING UP STITCHES AROUND NECK.

SIZES: 1 YEAR (2 YEAR, 3 YEAR)

KNITTED MEASUREMENTS: WIDTH = 12″ (13″, 15″), LENGTH = 12″ (13½″, 15″), SLEEVE LENGTH = 7″ (8″, 10″)

FINISHING:

Sew shoulder seams together. Sew sleeves on to body and then sew up side and sleeve seams. With a circular 16″ #11 circular needle, pick up 36 (42, 42) stitches around the neck. Work in garter/rib pattern as follows: Row 1: Knit. Row 2: K3, P3 across row. Repeat rows 1 and 2 for 1″. Bind off all stitches loosely.

Remember that after binding off the center stitches, you will work one side at a time.

1-YEAR SIZE

ROW 1: Work 16 stitches; with the 15th stitch, begin to bind off the center 9 stitches. This means you should pull the 15th stitch over the 16th stitch, and this is your first bind-off. When you are done binding off the center 9 stitches, check to make sure you have 14 stitches on each side of the hole, including the stitch on the right-hand needle. Continue P2, K3, P3, K3, P2. Turn work.

ROW 2: Purl. Turn work.

ROW 3: Bind off 3 stitches. K2, P3, K3, P2. Turn work.

ROW 4: Purl. Turn work.

ROW 5: Bind off 1 stitch. K1, P3, K3, P2. Turn work.

ROW 6: Purl. Turn work.

ROW 7: Bind off 1 stitch. P3, K3, P2. Turn work.

ROW 8: Purl.

2-YEAR AND 3-YEAR SIZES

ROW 1: Work 16 (19) stitches; with the 15th (18th) stitch, begin to bind off the center 11 stitches. This means you should pull the 15th (18th) stitch over the 16th (19th) stitch, and this is your first bind-off. When you are done binding off the center 11 stitches, check to make sure you have 14 (17) stitches on each side of the hole, including the stitch on the right-hand needle. Continue for size 2: K1, P3, K3, P3, K3; for size 3: P1, K3, P3, K3, P3, K3. Turn work.

ROW 2: Purl. Turn work.

ROW 3: Bind off 3 stitches. Size 2: P1, K3, P3, K3; Size 3: K1, P3, K3, P3, K3. Turn work.

ROW 4: Purl. Turn work.

ROW 5: Bind off 1 stitch. Size 2: K3, P3, K3; Size 3: P3, K3, P3, K3. Turn work.

ROW 6: Purl. Turn work.

ROW 7: Bind off 1 stitch. Size 2: K2, P3, K3; Size 3: P2, K3, P3, K3. Turn work.

ROW 8: Purl.

• For the other side of the neck edge, attach yarn to the remaining stitches and begin binding off 3 stitches immediately. You will now be binding off when you are purling. Finish neck shaping as on other side and bind off remaining stitches.

• When you are done with the bind-off instructions, compare the length of the front piece to the length of the back. If the front and back measure the same, bind off the remaining stitches. If the front is too short, continue knitting and purling until the pieces are of equal length, then bind off.

this is it!, for him

Note: To increase as a purl, work the bar method as you would if you were increasing as a knit, but purl the loop instead of knitting it. And remember, the increases come every 4th row.

1-YEAR AND 2-YEAR SIZES

ROW 1: K2 *(K3, P3)* to last 2 stitches, K2. Turn work.

ROW 2: Purl. Turn work.

ROW 3: As row 1. Turn work.

ROW 4: Purl. Turn work.

ROW 1: K2, increase as a purl, *(K3, P3)* to last 2 stitches, increase as a knit, K2. Turn work.

ROW 2: Purl. Turn work.

ROW 3: K2, P1 *(K3, P3)* to last 3 stitches, K3. Turn work.

ROW 4: Purl. Turn work.

ROW 1: K2, increase as a purl, P1 *(K3, P3)* to last 3 stitches, K1, increase as a knit, K2. Turn work.

ROW 2: Purl. Turn work.

ROW 3: K2, P2 *(K3, P3)* to last 4 stitches, K4. Turn work.

ROW 4: Purl. Turn work.

Always leaving 2 knit stitches on either end of every RS row, continue increasing in this way, taking new stitches in the K3, P3 pattern until the correct number of stitches is reached. For example: After you have increased as a purl 3 times at the beginning of an increase row and as a knit at the end of the increase row, you will reverse this. You will continue by knitting 2 stitches, increasing as a knit, then work in pattern to last 2 stitches, increasing as a purl, and knitting 2. You will work this way for 3 consecutive increase rows, and then you will reverse the increase order again.

3-YEAR SIZE

ROW 1: K2, *(K3, P3)* to last 5 stitches, K5. Turn work.

ROW 2: Purl. Turn work.

ROW 3: As row 1. Turn work.

ROW 4: Purl. Turn work.

ROW 1: K2, increase as a purl, *(K3, P3)* to last 5 stitches, K3, increase as a purl, K2. Turn work.

ROW 2: Purl. Turn work.

ROW 3: K2, P1 *(K3, P3)* to last 6 stitches, K3, P1, K2. Turn work.

ROW 4: Purl. Turn work.

ROW 1: K2, increase as a purl, P1 *(K3, P3)* to last 6 stitches, K3, P1, increase as a purl, K2. Turn work.

ROW 2: Purl. Turn work.

ROW 3: K2, P2 *(K3, K3)* to last 7 stitches, K3, P2, K2. Turn work.

ROW 4: Purl. Turn work.

Always leaving 2 knit stitches on either end of every RS row, continue increasing in this way, taking new stitches in the K3, P3 pattern until the correct number of stitches is reached. For example: After you have increased as a purl 3 times at the beginning and end of an increase row, you will reverse this. You will continue by knitting 2 stitches, increasing as a knit, then work in pattern to last 2 stitches, increasing as a knit, and knitting 2. You will work this way for 3 consecutive increase rows, and then you will increase as a purl for 3 consecutive increase rows.

even daniele did it, again

Baby sweaters are perfect to knit when trying out new techniques. Daniele had pretty much mastered simple stockinette sweaters and was ready to move on to something a little more challenging. With her reputation as a spaz knitter well behind her, she decided she wanted to play with color. We encouraged her to make this sweater because not only could she choose fun colors but also she could learn how to knit stripes. Daniele chose beautiful colors for her friend's baby girl and picked up striping in a flash. She enjoyed making this sweater so much she chose other colors and made the same sweater for her nephew.

BACK:

With #7 needle and color A, cast on 40 (44, 48, 54, 60) stitches. Work in K1, P1 ribbing for 4 rows. Change to #9 needle and work in St st until piece measures 3″ (3½″, 3¾″, 4½″, 5″), ending with a purl row. Purl 1 row on a RS row. Change to color B. Work in St st for 3″ (3½″, 3¾″, 4½″, 5″), ending with a purl row. Purl 1 row on a RS row. Change to color C. Work 3″ (3½″, 3¾″, 4½″, 5″) in St st, ending with a purl row. Purl 1 row on a RS row. Bind off all stitches. The back should measure approximately 10″ (11″, 12″, 13½″, 15″).

FRONT:

Work as for back until piece measures 8″ (9″, 9½″, 11″, 12½″) from cast-on edge, ending with a WS row. **Shape Crew Neck:** Bind off center 10 (12, 12, 14, 14) and then begin working each side of the neck separately. At the beginning of each neck edge, every other row, bind off 3 stitches 1 time, 2 stitches 1 time, 1 stitch 2 times. (See step-by-step instructions.) Continue to work as for back on remaining 8 (9, 11, 13, 16) stitches with no further decreasing until piece measures same as back. Bind off all stitches loosely.

SLEEVES:

With #7 needle and color A, cast on 24 (26, 28, 30, 30) stitches. Work in K1, P1 ribbing for 4 rows. Change to #9 needle and work in St st, making color changes as you did for the back. When sleeve measures 2″ (2¼″, 2½″, 2¾″, 3¼″), purl 1 row on a RS row. Change to color B. Work in St st in color B for 2″ (2¼″, 2½″, 2¾″, 3¼″). Purl 1 row on RS row. Change to color C. **AT THE SAME TIME,** increase 1 stitch at each edge every 4th row 6 (7, 9, 9, 11) times until you have 36 (40, 46, 48, 52) stitches.

NOTE: INCREASE LEAVING 2 EDGE STITCHES ON EITHER SIDE OF WORK. THIS MEANS YOU SHOULD KNIT 2 STITCHES, INCREASE 1 STITCH, KNIT TO THE LAST 2 STITCHES, INCREASE 1 STITCH, AND THEN KNIT THE 2 REMAINING STITCHES. INCREASING LIKE THIS MAKES IT EASIER TO SEW UP YOUR SEAMS.

When sleeve measures approximately 6″ (6¾″, 7½″, 8½″, 9¾″), work 1 purl row on the RS. Bind off all stitches loosely.

FINISHING:

Sew shoulder seams together. Sew sleeves on and sew up sleeve and side seams. With a circular 16″ #7 needle and color A, pick up 60 (62, 64, 66, 68) stitches around the neck. Work in K1, P1 ribbing for 6 rows. Bind off all stitches loosely.

YARN: MANOS DEL URUGUAY (138 YARDS / 100G BALL)

FIBER CONTENT: 100% HANDSPUN PURE WOOL

COLORS:
GIRL VERSION: A-66 (RED), B-47 (PINK), C-W (ORANGE)
BOY VERSION: A-8 (BLACK), B-59 (GRAY), C-K (OFF-WHITE)

AMOUNT: 1 (1, 2, 2, 2) BALL(S) COLOR A; 1 (1, 1, 2, 2) BALL(S) COLOR B, 1 (1, 1, 2, 2) BALL(S) COLOR C

TOTAL YARDAGE: 414 (414, 552, 828, 828) YARDS

GAUGE: 4 STITCHES = 1 INCH; 16 STITCHES = 4 INCHES

NEEDLE SIZE: US #9 (5.5MM) FOR BODY OR SIZE NEEDED TO OBTAIN GAUGE; US #7 (4.5MM) FOR RIBBING; CIRCULAR 16″ US #7 (4.5MM) FOR PICKING UP STITCHES AROUND NECK

SIZES: 0–3 MONTHS (3–6 MONTHS, 1 YEAR, 2 YEAR, 3 YEAR)

KNITTED MEASUREMENTS: WIDTH = 10″ (11″, 12″, 13½″, 15″), LENGTH =10″ (11″, 12″, 13½″, 15″), SLEEVE LENGTH = 6″ (6¾″, 7½″, 8½″, 9¾″)

STEP-BY-STEP GUIDE TO SHAPING THE CREW NECK

Remember that after binding off the center stitches, you will work one side at a time.

ROW 1: Knit 17 (18, 20, 22, 25) stitches; with the 16th (17th, 19th, 21st, 24th) stitch begin to bind off the center 10 (12, 12, 14, 14) stitches. For example, for the 0–3 month-size, this means you should pull the 16th stitch over the 17th stitch, and this is your first bind-off. When you are done binding off the center 10 (12, 12, 14, 14) stitches, check to make sure you have 15 (16, 18, 20, 23) stitches on each side of the hole, including the stitch on the right-hand needle. Knit to end of row. Turn work.

ROW 2: Purl. Turn work.

ROW 3: Bind off first 3 stitches. Knit to end of row. Turn work.

ROW 4: Purl. Turn work.

ROW 5: Bind off first 2 stitches. Knit to end of row. Turn work.

ROW 6: Purl. Turn work.

ROW 7: Bind off 1 stitch. Knit to end of row. Turn work.

ROW 8: Purl. Turn work.

ROW 9: Bind off 1 stitch. Knit to end of row. Turn work.

ROW 10: Purl.

• For the other side of the neck edge, attach yarn to the remaining stitches and begin binding off 3 stitches immediately. You will now be binding off when you are purling. Finish neck shaping as on other side and bind off remaining stitches.

• When you are done with the bind-off instructions, compare the length of the front piece to the length of the back. If the front and back measure the same, bind off the remaining stitches. If the front is too short, continue knitting and purling until the pieces are of equal length, then bind off.

even daniele did it again, for her

basic
cardigans

For many reasons, cardigans are always a popular choice for baby projects. You don't have to wrestle them over your little one's head. You can button and unbutton them easily on those days when it's warm one minute and chilly the next. But best of all, you get to choose fun buttons. And if you don't know the sex of the child for whom you are knitting, you can wait until the very last minute to pick out buttons to add a girl or boy spin on an otherwise androgynous sweater.

The projects in this chapter are all very simple cardigans. *Like Riding a Bike* is as basic as it gets: simple ribbing around all edges, straight stockinette stitch otherwise. It's made with super-chunky yarn so it can be worn in the dead of winter under a warm coat or on milder days as a jacket. *Triple the Fun* is a little different than the basic cardigan because it has a hood and the button bands are knit into the front panels of the sweater. This is an especially great feature for those of you who dislike or are just plain intimidated by picking up stitches. Finally, *Cute as a Button* is a simple stockinette cardigan with a collar and a crochet border. Using a contrasting color for the border makes the sweater a little more fun than sticking to one solid color for the whole thing—but if you want to stay sophisticated, you can do that too.

like riding a bike

Karen, a regular customer, came into our shop with her pregnant friend Paula. They had been out to lunch and Karen had a few questions about her project and persuaded Paula to come along. As Paula was sitting around waiting for Karen to get help, her maternal instincts kicked in and she got inspired by all the baby sweaters hanging up. She asked us about our beginner classes but she also mentioned she had learned to knit in camp when she was 12 years old. We told her that a class probably wouldn't be necessary because for most people knitting is like riding a bike. Once someone quickly shows you, it comes right back. We sat with her for about 2 minutes and reminded her how to knit and purl. She wanted to make the easiest cardigan we could think of. This is what we came up with.

YARN: TAHKI, BABY (60 YARDS / 100G BALL)

FIBER CONTENT: 100% MERINO WOOL

COLORS:
GIRL VERSION: 41
BOY VERSION: 32

AMOUNT: 4 (5, 6) BALLS

TOTAL YARDAGE: 240 (300, 360) YARDS

GAUGE: 2 STITCHES = 1 INCH; 8 STITCHES = 4 INCHES

NEEDLE SIZE: US #15 (10MM) FOR BODY OR SIZE NEEDED TO OBTAIN GAUGE; US #13 (9MM) FOR RIBBING

SIZES: 1 YEAR (2 YEAR, 3 YEAR)

KNITTED MEASUREMENTS: WIDTH = 12" (14", 15"), LENGTH = 12" (13½", 15"), SLEEVE LENGTH = 7" (8", 10")

OTHER MATERIALS: 5 BUTTONS

BACK:

With #13 needle, cast on 24 (28, 32) stitches. Work in K2, P2 ribbing for 4 rows. Change to #15 needle and work in St st until piece measures 12" (13½", 15") from cast-on edge, ending with a WS row. Bind off all stitches loosely.

FRONT: (make 2, reverse shaping)

With #13 needle, cast on 12 (14, 16) stitches. Work in K2, P2 ribbing for 4 rows as follows: For 1-year and 3-year sizes: K2, P2 for 4 rows. For 2-year sizes: Row 1: K2 *(K2, P2)* to end. Row 2: P2 *(K2, P2)* to end. Repeat rows 1 and 2. Change to #15 needle and work in St st until piece measures 9½" (11", 12½") from cast-on edge, ending with a WS row. **Shape Crew Neck:** At beginning of each neck edge, every other row, bind off 2 (2, 3) stitches once, 1 stitch 3 times. (See step-by-step instructions.) Continue to work in St st on remaining 7 (9, 10) stitches until piece measures 12" (13½", 15") from cast-on edge, ending with a WS row. Bind off all stitches loosely.

SLEEVES:

With #13 needle, cast on 14 (14, 16) stitches. Work in K2, P2 ribbing for 4 rows as follows: For 1-year and 2-year sizes: Row 1: K2 *(P2, K2)* to end. Row 2: P2 *(K2, P2)* to end. Repeat rows 1 and 2. For 3-year size: K2, P2 for 4 rows. Change to #15 needle and work in St st. **AT THE SAME TIME,** increase 1 stitch at each edge every 4th row 4 (5, 5) times until you have 22 (24, 26) stitches.

NOTE: INCREASE LEAVING 2 EDGE STITCHES ON EITHER SIDE. THIS MEANS YOU SHOULD KNIT 2 STITCHES, INCREASE 1 STITCH, KNIT TO THE LAST 2 STITCHES, INCREASE 1 STITCH, AND THEN KNIT THE REMAINING 2 STITCHES. INCREASING LIKE THIS MAKES IT EASIER TO SEW UP YOUR SEAMS.

When sleeve measures 7" (8", 10") from cast-on edge, ending with a WS row, bind off all stitches loosely.

FINISHING:

Sew shoulder seams together. Sew sleeves on. Sew up side and sleeve seams. With #13 needle and RS facing, pick up 30 (30, 32) stitches around the neck edge for collar. Work in K2, P2 ribbing for 4 rows as follows: For

1-year and 2-year sizes: Row 1: K2 *(P2, K2)* to end. Row 2: P2 *(K2, P2)* to end. Repeat rows 1 and 2. For 3-year size: K2, P2 for 4 rows. Bind off all stitches loosely.

Button band: With RS facing and #13 needle, pick up 26 (30, 34) stitches. Work 4 rows as follows for all sizes: Row 1: K2 *(P2, K2)* to end. Row 2: P2 *(K2, P2)* to end. Repeat rows 1 and 2. Bind off all stitches loosely.

Buttonhole band: With RS facing and #13 needle, pick up 26 (30, 34) stitches. Work 4 rows as follows for all sizes: Row 1: K2 *(P2, K2)* to end. Row 2: Rib 2 (YO, rib 2tog, rib 3, 4, 5) 4 times, end rib 2tog, YO, rib 2. Row 3: K2 *(P2, K2)* to end. Row 4: P2 *(K2, P2)* to end. Bind off loosely.

NOTE: FOR GIRLS, BUTTONHOLES GO ON THE RIGHT SIDE; FOR BOYS, BUTTONHOLES GO ON THE LEFT SIDE. THIS IS AS THE SWEATER IS WORN, NOT AS YOU KNIT IT.

like riding a bike, for him

LEFT FRONT
(left side when worn)

ROW 1: Bind off 2 (2, 3) stitches. Purl to end. Turn work.

ROW 2: Knit. Turn work.

ROW 3: Bind off 1 stitch. Purl to end. Turn work.

ROW 4: Knit. Turn work.

Repeat rows 3 and 4 twice more.

RIGHT FRONT
(right side when worn)

ROW 1: Bind off 2 (2, 3) stitches. Knit to end. Turn work.

ROW 2: Purl. Turn work.

ROW 3: Bind off 1 stitch. Knit to end. Turn work.

ROW 4: Purl. Turn work.

Repeat rows 3 and 4 twice more.

• When you are done with the bind-off instructions, compare the length of the front piece to the length of the back. If the front and the back measure the same, bind off the remaining stitches.

triple the fun

In addition to working at our shop part-time, Maureen also has a full-time job. As you can imagine, she doesn't have a lot of time to knit. But she loves to knit matching sweaters for her triplet nephews, which she does once a year. She always gets upset when they grow out of them quickly, and she hates that the sweaters are worn for such a short time. So we came up with a hooded cardigan for the kids to wear fall, winter, and spring.

BACK:

With #9 needle and 2 strands of yarn, cast on 40 (44, 48, 54, 60) stitches. Work in garter stitch for 6 rows. Then work in St st until piece measures 10" (11", 12", 13½", 15") from cast-on edge, ending with a WS row. Bind off all stitches loosely.

NOTE: BUTTONHOLES FOR THE BOY VERSION ARE MADE ON THE LEFT FRONT AS WORN, NOT AS YOU KNIT. FOR THE GIRL VERSION, THE BUTTONHOLES ARE MADE ON THE RIGHT FRONT. WE SUGGEST YOU DO THE SIDE WITHOUT THE BUTTONHOLES FIRST.

TO MAKE THE BUTTONHOLES FOR BOYS: ON A RS ROW, KNIT UNTIL 4 STITCHES BEFORE THE END OF THE ROW, K2TOG, YO, K2. FOR GIRLS: ON RS ROW, K2, YO, K2TOG, KNIT UNTIL END.

LEFT FRONT:

With #9 needle and 2 strands of yarn, cast on 23 (25, 27, 30, 33) stitches. Work in garter stitch for 6 rows. Then work as follows: Row 1: Knit. Row 2: K5, purl to end. Continue working rows 1 and 2 until piece measures 8" (9", 9½", 11", 12½") from cast-on edge, ending with a RS row. **Shape Crew Neck:** At beginning of each neck edge, every other row, bind off 5 stitches once, 4 stitches once, 3 stitches once, 2 stitches once, 1 stitch 0 (1, 1, 1, 2) times. (See step-by-step instructions.) Continue in St

st on remaining 9 (10, 12, 15, 17) stitches until piece measures 10" (11", 12", 13½", 15") from cast-on edge, ending with a WS row. Bind off all stitches loosely. **FOR BOY VERSION:** Place buttonholes at ½", then every 1¾" (2", 2", 2½", 2¾").

RIGHT FRONT:

With #9 needle and 2 strands of yarn, cast on 23 (25, 27, 30, 33) stitches. Work in garter stitch for 6 rows. Then work as follows: Row 1: Knit. Row 2: Purl until 5 stitches remain, K5. Continue working rows 1 and 2 until piece measures 8" (9", 9½", 11", 12½") from cast-on edge, ending with a WS row. **Shape Crew Neck:** At beginning of each neck edge, every other row, bind off 5 stitches once, 4 stitches once, 3 stitches once, 2 stitches once, 1 stitch 0 (1, 1, 1, 2) times. (See step-by-step instructions.) Continue in St st on remaining 9 (10, 12, 15, 17) stitches until piece measures 10" (11", 12", 13½", 15") from cast-on edge, ending with a WS row. Bind off all stitches loosely. **FOR GIRL VERSION:** Place buttonholes at ½", then every 1¾" (2", 2", 2½", 2¾").

YARN: KOIGU WOOL DESIGNS (175 YARDS / 50G BALL)

FIBER CONTENT: 100% MERINO WOOL

COLORS:
GIRL VERSION: P831
BOY VERSION: P400

AMOUNT: 4 (4, 5, 6, 7) BALLS

TOTAL YARDAGE: 700 (700, 875, 1050, 1225) YARDS

GAUGE: 4 STITCHES = 1 INCH; 16 STITCHES = 4 INCHES

NEEDLE SIZE: US #9 (5.5MM) OR SIZE NEEDED TO OBTAIN GAUGE

SIZES: 0–3 MONTHS (3–6 MONTHS, 1 YEAR, 2 YEAR, 3 YEAR)

KNITTED MEASUREMENTS: WIDTH = 10" (11", 12", 13½", 15"), LENGTH =10" (11", 12", 13½", 15"), SLEEVE LENGTH = 6" (6½", 7", 8", 10")

OTHER MATERIALS: 5 BUTTONS

Yarn is worked double throughout the sweater—this means you should hold 2 strands of yarn together as though they are 1.

SLEEVES:

With #9 needle and 2 strands of yarn, cast on 24 (24, 28, 30, 32) stitches. Work in garter stitch for 6 rows. Work in St st. **AT THE SAME TIME,** increase 1 stitch at each edge every 4th row 6 (8, 8, 10, 10) times until you have 36 (40, 44, 50, 52) stitches.

NOTE: INCREASE LEAVING 2 EDGE STITCHES ON EITHER SIDE. THIS MEANS YOU SHOULD KNIT 2 STITCHES, INCREASE 1 STITCH, KNIT TO THE LAST 2 STITCHES, INCREASE 1 STITCH, AND KNIT THE REMAINING 2 STITCHES. INCREASING LIKE THIS MAKES IT EASIER TO SEW UP YOUR SEAMS.

Continue in St st until sleeve measures 6" (6½", 7", 8", 10") from the cast-on edge, ending with a WS row. Bind off all stitches loosely.

HOOD:

With #9 needle and 2 strands of yarn, cast on 24 (26, 30, 32, 36) stitches. Work as follows: Row 1: Knit. Row 2: K5, purl to end. Work these 2 rows until hood measures 16″ (18″, 20″, 22″, 22″) from cast-on edge, ending with a WS row. Bind off all stitches loosely.

FINISHING:

Sew shoulder seams together. Sew sleeves on. Sew up side and sleeve seams. Fold hood in half and sew down the back side (the side without the garter-stitch border). Then sew hood onto sweater starting at the middle of the back of the neck and ending at the end of the garter-stitch button band.

triple the fun, for her

STEP-BY-STEP GUIDE TO SHAPING THE CREW NECK

LEFT FRONT
(left side when worn)

ROW 1: Bind off 5 stitches. Purl to end. Turn work.

ROW 2: Knit. Turn work.

ROW 3: Bind off 4 stitches. Purl to end. Turn work.

ROW 4: Knit. Turn work.

ROW 5: Bind off 3 stitches. Purl to end. Turn work.

ROW 6: Knit. Turn work.

ROW 7: Bind off 2 stitches. Purl to end. Turn work.

ROW 8: Knit. Turn work.

You are now done with neck shaping for the 0–3 month size. For other sizes, continue as follows:

ROW 10: Bind off 1 stitch. Purl to end. Turn work.

ROW 11: Knit. Turn work.

Repeat rows 9 and 10 once more for the 3-year size only.

RIGHT FRONT
(right side when worn)

ROW 1: Bind off 5 stitches. Knit to end. Turn work.

ROW 2: Purl. Turn work.

ROW 3: Bind off 4 stitches. Knit to end. Turn work.

ROW 4: Purl. Turn work.

ROW 5: Bind off 3 stitches. Knit to end. Turn work.

ROW 6: Purl. Turn work.

ROW 7: Bind off 2 stitches. Knit to end. Turn work.

ROW 8: Purl. Turn work.

You are now done with neck shaping for the 0–3 month size. For other sizes, continue as follows:

ROW 10: Bind off 1 stitch. Knit to end. Turn work.

ROW 11: Purl. Turn work.

Repeat rows 9 and 10 once more for the 3-year size only.

• When you are done with the bind-off instructions, compare the length of the front piece to the length of the back. If the front and the back measure the same, bind off the remaining stitches.

Cute as a button

Sometimes you find buttons before you even think about making a sweater. You see them and you know that you must have them. Who knows when you will use them—but they are just too cute or too beautiful to pass up. So you buy them and put them away for a while, knowing that eventually you will find the perfect project for them. This is what happened to Julie. Her good friend found out she was having a girl. Julie wanted to make something special quickly. She remembered these buttons that were hidden away and decided to design a cardigan for them. The sweater had to be simple so as not to take away from the buttons, and the yarn had to come in a variety of colors so Julie could find a color to match the buttons. This design has been one of our most popular baby cardigans ever since. Some people choose the buttons first, like Julie did, while others choose wonderful colors and then find buttons to match. Either way, the sweater knits up in a jiffy, it looks great on boys and girls, and everybody loves it!

BACK:

With #10½ needle and 2 strands of color A, cast on 42 (48, 52) stitches. Work in St st until piece measures 12″ (13½″, 15″) from cast-on edge, ending with a WS row. Bind off all stitches loosely.

FRONT: (make 2, reverse shaping)

With #10½ needle and 2 strands of color A, cast on 22 (25, 27) stitches. Work in St st until piece measures 9½″ (11″, 12½″) from cast-on edge, ending with a WS row. **Shape Crew Neck:** At beginning of each neck edge, every other row, bind off 4 stitches once, 3 stitches once, 2 stitches once, 1 stitch 1 (2, 2) time. (See step-by-step instructions.) Continue to work in St st on remaining 12 (14, 16) stitches until piece measures 12″ (13½″, 15″) from cast-on edge, ending with a WS row. Bind off all stitches loosely.

SLEEVES:

With #10½ needle and 2 strands of color A, cast on 22 (26, 28) stitches. Work in St st. **AT THE SAME TIME,** increase 1 stitch at each edge every 4th (4th, 6th) row 8 times until you have 38 (42, 44) stitches.

NOTE: INCREASE LEAVING 2 EDGE STITCHES ON EITHER SIDE. THIS MEANS YOU SHOULD KNIT 2 STITCHES, INCREASE 1 STITCH, KNIT TO THE LAST 2 STITCHES, INCREASE 1 STITCH, AND THEN KNIT THE REMAINING 2 STITCHES. INCREASING LIKE THIS MAKES IT EASIER TO SEW UP YOUR SEAMS.

When sleeve measures 7″ (8″, 10″) from cast-on edge, ending with a WS row, bind off all stitches loosely.

FINISHING:

Sew shoulder seams together. Sew sleeves on. Sew up side and sleeve seams. With #10½ needle, 2 strands of color A, and WS facing you, pick up 36 (38, 42) stitches around the neck edge for collar. Work in St st, beginning with a purl row, for 4″. Bind off all stitches loosely.

YARN: FILATURA DI CROSA, ZARA (136 YARDS / 50G BALL)

FIBER CONTENT: 100% MERINO WOOL

COLORS:
GIRL VERSION: A-1668, B-1660
BOY VERSION: A-1389, B-1468

AMOUNT: 5 (6, 8) BALLS COLOR A; 1 BALL COLOR B

TOTAL YARDAGE: 680 (816, 1088) YARDS COLOR A; 136 YARDS COLOR B

GAUGE: 3½ STITCHES = 1 INCH; 14 STITCHES = 4 INCHES

NEEDLE SIZE: US #10½ (7MM) OR SIZE NEEDED TO OBTAIN GAUGE; J CROCHET HOOK

SIZES: 1 YEAR (2 YEAR, 3 YEAR)

KNITTED MEASUREMENTS: WIDTH = 12″ (13½″, 15″), LENGTH = 12″ (13½″, 15″), SLEEVE LENGTH = 7″ (8″, 10″)

OTHER MATERIALS: 5 BUTTONS

Yarn is worked double throughout the sweater—this means you should hold 2 strands of yarn together as though they are 1.

Crochet Border: You will crochet in 3 parts: First you will crochet the collar, then all around the fronts and the bottom, and finally the cuffs. With a J crochet hook, 2 strands of color B, and the RS of the collar facing you, work 1 row of single crochet and 1 row of shrimp stitch.

Space 5 markers evenly on the right side for a girl and the left for a boy. When crocheting the sides, make 2 extra chains when you come to these buttonhole markers. Then, with RS facing at the top of the left front of the sweater, single crochet 1 row down left side, across bottom, up right side. Then shrimp stitch down right side, across bottom, and up left side.

Single crochet and shrimp stitch along cuff borders.

LEFT FRONT (left side when worn)	RIGHT FRONT (right side when worn)
ROW 1: Bind off 4 stitches. Purl to end. Turn work.	ROW 1: Bind off 4 stitches. Knit to end. Turn work.
ROW 2: Knit. Turn work.	ROW 2: Purl. Turn work.
ROW 3: Bind off 3 stitches. Purl to end. Turn work.	ROW 3: Bind off 3 stitches. Knit to end. Turn work.
ROW 4: Knit. Turn work.	ROW 4: Purl. Turn work.
ROW 5: Bind off 2 stitches. Purl to end. Turn work.	ROW 5: Bind off 2 stitches. Knit to end. Turn work.
ROW 6: Knit. Turn work.	ROW 6: Purl. Turn work.
ROW 7: Bind off 1 stitch. Purl to end. Turn work.	ROW 7: Bind off 1 stitch. Knit to end. Turn work.
ROW 8: Knit. Turn work.	ROW 8: Purl. Turn work.
For 2-year and 3-year sizes, repeat rows 7 and 8 once more.	For 2-year and 3-year sizes, repeat rows 7 and 8 once more.

• When you are done with the bind-off instructions, compare the length of the front piece to the length of the back. If the front and the back measure the same, bind off the remaining stitches.

HINT: To determine where to insert crochet hook on the single crochet row: When you are crocheting up or down rows (that is, on the sides of the collar or button bands), insert crochet hook into every other row (or hole). When crocheting across stitches (across top of collar, along bottom of sweater, or along sleeves), insert hook every stitch and a half, which is the same as every 3rd hole.

cute as a button, for her

beyond basic
cardigans

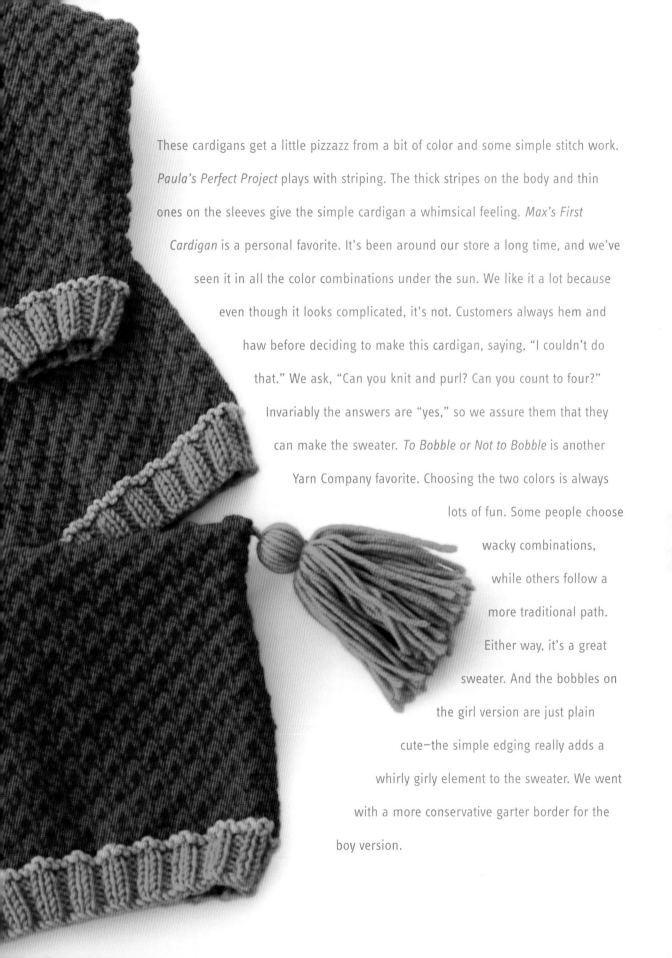

These cardigans get a little pizzazz from a bit of color and some simple stitch work. *Paula's Perfect Project* plays with striping. The thick stripes on the body and thin ones on the sleeves give the simple cardigan a whimsical feeling. *Max's First Cardigan* is a personal favorite. It's been around our store a long time, and we've seen it in all the color combinations under the sun. We like it a lot because even though it looks complicated, it's not. Customers always hem and haw before deciding to make this cardigan, saying, "I couldn't do that." We ask, "Can you knit and purl? Can you count to four?" Invariably the answers are "yes," so we assure them that they can make the sweater. *To Bobble or Not to Bobble* is another Yarn Company favorite. Choosing the two colors is always lots of fun. Some people choose wacky combinations, while others follow a more traditional path. Either way, it's a great sweater. And the bobbles on the girl version are just plain cute—the simple edging really adds a whirly girly element to the sweater. We went with a more conservative garter border for the boy version.

paula's perfect project

Paula was in the habit of making sweaters for herself and then ripping them out. She always found something wrong with them: too tight here, too loose there, it made her bust look too small, it made her butt look too big, or the color made her skin look sallow. These were all imaginary problems—the sweaters all looked great on her—but what could we do? Well, we suggested she stop making sweaters for herself and focus on the many babies her friends all seemed to be having. She ripped out two sweaters in different colors she had made in Capri, and then we designed this cute stripy cardigan. She made several of them, and they came out perfectly. None of the babies complained a bit about the length, the width, or the color.

YARN: TAHKI, CAPRI (52 YARDS / 50G BALL)

FIBER CONTENT: 100% EGYPTIAN COTTON

COLORS:
GIRL VERSION: A-05, B-09
BOY VERSION: A-08, B-01

AMOUNT: 4 (5, 5) BALLS COLOR A; 2 (3, 3) BALLS COLOR B

TOTAL YARDAGE: 312 (416, 416) YARDS

GAUGE: 3 STITCHES = 1 INCH; 12 STITCHES = 4 INCHES

NEEDLE SIZE: US #13 (9MM) FOR BODY OR SIZE NEEDED TO OBTAIN GAUGE; US #11 (8MM) FOR RIBBING

SIZES: 1 YEAR (2 YEAR, 3 YEAR)

KNITTED MEASUREMENTS: WIDTH = 12" (13½", 15"), LENGTH = 12" (13½", 15"), SLEEVE LENGTH = 7" (8", 10")

OTHER MATERIALS: 5 BUTTONS

STRIPED ST ST #1:
6 rows color B,
6 rows color A

STRIPED ST ST #2:
2 rows color B,
2 rows color A

BACK:

With #11 needle and color A, cast on 36 (40, 44) stitches. Work in K2, P2 ribbing for 6 rows. Change to #13 needle and work in Striped St st #1 until piece measures 12" (13½", 15") from cast-on edge, ending with a WS row. Bind off all stitches loosely.

FRONT: (make 2, reverse shaping)

With #11 needle and color A, cast on 18 (20, 22) stitches. Work in K2, P2 ribbing for 6 rows as follows: For 1-year and 3-year sizes: Row 1: K2 *(P2, K2)* to end. Row 2: P2 *(K2, P2)*. Repeat rows 1 and 2 twice more. For 2-year size: K2, P2 for 6 rows. Change to #13 needle and work in Striped St st #1 until piece measures 9½" (11", 12½") from cast-on edge. **Shape Crew Neck:** At beginning of neck edge, every other row, bind off 3 stitches 1 time, 2 stitches 1 time, 1 stitch 2 (3, 3) times. (See step-by-step instructions.) Continue in Striped St st #1 on remaining 11 (12, 14) stitches until piece measures 12" (13½", 15") from cast-on edge, ending with a WS row. Bind off all stitches loosely.

SLEEVES:

With #11 needle and color A, cast on 20 (22, 22) stitches. Work in K2, P2 ribbing for 6 rows as follows: 1-year size: K2, P2 for 6 rows. For 2-year and 3-year sizes: Row 1: K2 (*P2, K2*) to end. Row 2: P2 (*K2, P2*) to end. Repeat rows 1 and 2 twice more. Change to #13 needle and work in Striped St st #2. **AT THE SAME TIME,** increase 1 stitch at each edge of every 4th row 7 (7, 9) times until you have 34 (36, 40) stitches.

NOTE: INCREASE LEAVING 2 EDGE STITCHES ON EITHER SIDE OF WORK. THIS MEANS YOU SHOULD KNIT 2 STITCHES, INCREASE 1 STITCH, AND THEN KNIT TO THE LAST 2 STITCHES, INCREASE 1 STITCH, AND THEN KNIT THE REMAINING 2 STITCHES. INCREASING LIKE THIS MAKES IT EASIER TO SEW UP YOUR SEAMS.

When sleeve measures 7" (8", 10") from cast-on edge, ending with a WS row, bind off all stitches loosely.

FINISHING:

Sew shoulder seams together. Sew sleeves to body. Sew up sleeve and side seams.

Neckband: With #11 needle, color A, and RS facing, pick up 36 (40, 40) stitches around the neck edge. Work in K2, P2 ribbing for 6 rows. Bind off all stitches loosely.

NOTE: BUTTONHOLES ARE PLACED ON THE RIGHT SIDE FOR GIRLS AND THE LEFT SIDE FOR BOYS. THIS IS AS THE SWEATER IS WORN, NOT AS IT IS KNIT.

Buttonhole band: With #11 needle, color A, and RS facing, pick up 36 (40, 46) stitches. For 1-year and 2-year sizes, work as follows: Rows 1 and 2: K2, P2. For 3-year size, work as follows: Row 1: K2 *(P2, K2)* to end. Row 2: P2 *(K2, P2)* to end. For all sizes: Row 3: Rib 3 (3, 2) (YO, Rib 2tog, Rib 5, 6, 8) 4 times, end Rib 2tog, YO, Rib 3 (3, 2). Then work Row 2 and Row 1 once more. Bind off all stitches loosely.

Button band: With #11 needle and RS facing, pick up 36 (40, 46) stitches for button band. For 1-year and 2-year sizes, work as follows: K2, P2 for 5 rows. For 3-year size, work as follows: Row 1: K2 *(P2, K2)* to end. Row 2: P2 *(K2, P2)* to end. Repeat rows 1 and 2, then row 1 again. Bind off loosely.

STEP-BY-STEP GUIDE TO SHAPING THE CREW NECK

LEFT FRONT
(left side when worn)

ROW 1: Bind off 3 stitches. Purl to end. Turn work.

ROW 2: Knit. Turn work.

ROW 3: Bind off 2 stitches. Purl to end. Turn work.

ROW 4: Knit. Turn work.

ROW 5: Bind off 1 stitch. Purl to end. Turn work.

ROW 6: Knit. Turn work.

Repeat rows 5 and 6 1 (2, 2) more time(s).

RIGHT FRONT
(right side when worn)

ROW 1: Bind off 3 stitches. Knit to end. Turn work.

ROW 2: Purl. Turn work.

ROW 3: Bind off 2 stitches. Knit to end. Turn work.

ROW 4: Purl. Turn work.

ROW 5: Bind off 1 stitch. Knit to end. Turn work.

ROW 6: Purl. Turn work.

Repeat rows 5 and 6 1 (2, 2) more time(s).

• When you are done with the bind-off instructions, compare the length of the front piece to the length of the back. If the front and the back measure the same, bind off the remaining stitches.

paula's perfect project, for her

max's first cardigan and hat

Jordana wrote this pattern more than five years ago, about

the time we bought the store. First she made it as a gift

for a friend; then she knitted it again as a sample for

the store. We hung it up and within days at least a dozen

people had decided to make it. Jordana still loves this sweater-

and-hat combo! It is the first thing she made for her

son, Max. She chose a heathered green body

(Dad has green eyes), an oatmeal color for

the accent, and a brownish color for the

ribbing. She also found the perfect

baseball buttons (Dad is a baseball

fanatic). Max started wearing the

sweater when he was a week old! He

had to wait a few weeks until the hat

fit, though.

YARN: FILATURA DI CROSA, ZARA (136 YARDS / 50G BALL)

FIBER CONTENT: 100% MERINO WOOL

COLORS:
GIRL VERSION: A-1704, B-1660, C-1501
BOY VERSION: A-6050, B-1472, C-1389

AMOUNT: 1 (1, 1, 1, 1) BALL COLOR A; 1 (1, 1, 1, 1) BALL COLOR B; 3 (4, 4, 5, 6) BALLS COLOR C

TOTAL YARDAGE: 136 (136, 136, 136, 136) YARDS COLOR A; 136 (136, 136, 136, 136) YARDS COLOR B; 408 (544, 544, 680, 816) YARDS COLOR C

GAUGE: 5 STITCHES = 1 INCH; 20 STITCHES = 4 INCHES

NEEDLE SIZE: US #7 (4.5MM) FOR BODY OR SIZE NEEDED TO OBTAIN GAUGE; US #5 (3.75MM) FOR RIBBING

SIZES: 0–3 MONTHS (3–6 MONTHS, 1 YEAR, 2 YEAR, 3 YEAR)

KNITTED MEASUREMENTS: WIDTH = 10½" (11", 12", 13½", 15"), LENGTH = 10" (11", 12", 13½", 15"), SLEEVE LENGTH = 6" (6½", 7", 8", 10")
HAT CIRCUMFERENCE: 14" (14¾", 15½", 16", 17")

OTHER MATERIALS: 5 BUTTONS

DOUBLE SEED STITCH:

If cast-on is divisible by 4:

ROWS 1 AND 2: **K2, P2.**

ROWS 3 AND 4: **P2, K2.**

If cast on is NOT divisible by 4:

ROW 1: **K2 *(P2, K2)* to end.**

ROW 2: **P2 *(K2, P2)* to end.**

ROW 3: **Repeat row 2.**

ROW 4: **Repeat row 1.**

cardigan

BACK:

With #5 needle and color A, cast on 52 (56, 60, 68, 76) stitches. Work in K2, P2 ribbing for 6 rows. Change to #7 needle and color B. Work 2 rows knit. Change to color C and work 1 row knit. Continue to work with color C in Double Seed Stitch until piece measures 10" (11", 12", 13½", 15") from cast-on edge, ending with a WS row. Bind off all stitches loosely.

FRONT: (make 2, reverse shaping)

With #5 needle and color A, cast on 26 (28, 30, 34, 38) stitches. Work in K2, P2 ribbing as follows for 6 rows: For 0–3 month, 1-year, 2-year, and 3-year sizes: Row 1: K2 * (P2, K2)* to end. Row 2: P2 * (K2, P2)* to end. Repeat rows 1 and 2 twice more. For 3–6 month size, K2, P2 for 6 rows. Change to #7 needle and color B. Work 2 rows of knit. Change to color C. Work 1 row in knit. Continue to work in color C in Double Seed Stitch until piece measures 8" (8½", 9½", 11", 12½") from cast-on edge. **Shape Crew Neck:** Keeping your Double Seed Stitch pattern correct, at beginning of each neck edge, every other row, bind off 4 stitches once, 3 stitches once, 2 stitches once, then 1 stitch 1 (1, 2, 3, 3) times. (See step-by-step instructions.) Continue to work in Double Seed Stitch on remaining 16 (17, 19, 22, 26) stitches until piece measures 10" (11", 12", 13½", 15") from cast-on edge, ending with a WS row. Bind off all stitches loosely.

SLEEVES:

With #5 needle and color A, cast on 30 (32, 36, 38, 40) stitches. Work in K2, P2 ribbing as follows for 6 rows: For 3–6 month, 1-year, and 3-year sizes: K2, P2 for 6 rows. For 0–3 month and 2-year sizes: Row 1: K2 *(P2, K2)* to end. Row 2: P2 *(K2, P2)* to end. Repeat rows 1 and 2 twice more. Change to #7 needle and color B. Work 2 rows in knit. Change to color C. Work 1 row in knit and then continue to work in Double Seed Stitch. **AT THE SAME TIME,** increase 1 stitch each edge every 4th row 9 (10, 10, 11, 12) times until you have 48 (52, 56, 60, 64) stitches.

NOTE: INCREASE LEAVING 2 EDGE STITCHES ON EITHER SIDE. THIS MEANS YOU SHOULD KNIT 2 STITCHES, INCREASE 1 STITCH WHILE KEEPING IN PATTERN, WORK IN DOUBLE SEED STITCH UNTIL 2 STITCHES REMAIN, INCREASE 1 STITCH IN PATTERN, AND THEN KNIT THE 2 REMAINING STITCHES. IT IS A LITTLE TRICKY BECAUSE THE STITCH YOU START WITH CHANGES EVERY 4 ROWS. (SEE STEP-BY-STEP INSTRUCTIONS.)

When sleeve measures 6" (6½", 7", 8", 10") from cast-on edge, ending with a WS row, bind off all stitches loosely.

FINISHING:

Sew shoulder seams together. Sew sleeves on. Sew up side and sleeve seams.

Neckband: With #5 needle, color B, and RS facing, pick up 48 (48, 54, 60, 62) stitches around the neck. Work 1 row of knit. Change to color A, work 1 row of knit, then work as follows: For 0–3-month, 3–6-month and 2-year sizes: K2, P2 for 6 rows. For 1-year and 3-year sizes: Row 1: K2 *(P2, K2)* to end. Row 2: P2 *(K2, P2)* to end. Repeat rows 1 and 2 twice more. Bind off loosely.

Buttonhole band: With #5 needle, color B, and RS facing, pick up 54 (56, 60, 66, 72) stitches. Work 1 row of knit. Change to color A and work 1 row of knit, then work as follows: For 1-year and 2-year sizes: K2, P2 for 2 rows. For 0–3-month, 3–6-month, and 3-year sizes: Row 1: K2 *(P2, K2)* to end. Row 2: P2 *(K2, P2)* to end. For all sizes. Row 3: Rib 2 (3, 3, 2, 3) (YO, Rib 2tog, Rib 10 (10, 11, 13, 14) 4 times, end Rib 2tog, YO, Rib 2 (3, 3, 2, 3). Work row 2 and then row 1 again. Bind off all stitches loosely.

Button band: Work as for buttonhole side, omitting buttonholes on row 3. Bind off all stitches loosely.

NOTE: BUTTONHOLES ARE PLACED ON THE RIGHT SIDE FOR GIRLS AND THE LEFT SIDE FOR BOYS. THIS IS AS THE SWEATER IS WORN, NOT AS IT IS KNIT.

hat

With #5 needle and color A, cast on 30 (30, 36, 38, 40) stitches. Work in K2, P2 ribbing for 6 rows as follows: For 0–3 month and 2-year sizes: Row 1: K2 *(P2, K2)* to end. Row 2: P2 *(K2, P2)* to end. Repeat rows 1 and 2 twice more. For 3–6 month, 1-year and 3-year sizes: K2, P2 every row. Change to #7 needle and color B. Work 2 rows in knit. Change to color C and work 1 row in knit. Continue to work with color C in Double Seed Stitch until piece measures 9″ (10″, 10½″, 11½″, 12½″) from cast-on edge, ending with a WS row. Change to color B and work 2 rows in knit. Change to #5 needle and color A and work 1 row in knit. Then work 6 rows in K2, P2 ribbing as follows: For 0–3 month and 2-year sizes: Row 1: K2 *(P2, K2)* to end. Row 2: P2 *(K2, P2)* to end. Repeat rows 1 and 2 twice more. For 3–6 month, 1-year and 3-year sizes: K2, P2 every row. Bind off loosely. Fold hat in half and sew side seams. Make 2 tassels and sew them to the top corners of the hat.

LEFT FRONT... when number of stitches cast on is NOT divisible by 4 (left side when worn). Begin bind-offs for neck edge on a row 1 of the pattern stitch.

ROW 1: Bind off 4 stitches. K1 *(P2, K2)* to end. Turn work.

ROW 2: As row 2 of pattern stitch. Turn work.

ROW 3: Bind off 3 stitches. P2 *(K2, P2)* to end. Turn work.

ROW 4: As row 4 of pattern stitch. Turn work.

ROW 5: Bind off 2 stitches. P2 *(K2, P2)* to end. Turn work.

ROW 6: As row 2 of pattern stitch. Turn work.

ROW 7: Bind off 1 stitch. K1, P2 *(K2, P2)* to end. Turn work.

ROW 8: As row 4 of pattern stitch. Turn work.

You are now done shaping the neck for the 0–3-month and the 3–6-month sizes.

ROW 9: Bind off 1 stitch. K2 *(P2, K2)* to end. Turn work.

ROW 10: As row 2 of pattern stitch. Turn work.

You are now done shaping the neck for the 1-year size.

ROW 11: Bind off 1 stitch. P1 *(K2, P2)* to end. Turn work.

ROW 12: As row 4 of pattern stitch.

You are now done shaping the neck for the 2-year and 3-year sizes.

LEFT FRONT ... when number of stitches cast on IS divisible by 4 (left side when worn). Begin bind-offs for neck edge on a row 1 of the pattern stitch.

ROW 1: Bind off 4 stitches. K1, P2 *(K2, P2)* to end. Turn work.

ROW 2: As row 2 of pattern stitch. Turn work.

ROW 3: Bind off 3 stitches. *(P2, K2)* to end. Turn work.

ROW 4: As row 4 of pattern stitch. Turn work.

ROW 5: Bind off 2 stitches. P2 *(K2, P2)* to end. Turn work.

ROW 6: As row 2 of pattern stitch. Turn work.

ROW 7: Bind off 1 stitch. K1 *(P2, K2)* to end. Turn work.

ROW 8: As row 4 of pattern stitch. Turn work.

You are now done shaping the neck for the 0–3-month and the 3–6-month sizes.

ROW 9: Bind off 1 stitch. *(K2, P2)* to end. Turn work.

ROW 10: As row 2 of pattern stitch. Turn work.

You are now done shaping the neck for the 1-year size.

ROW 11: Bind off 1 stitch. P1, K2 *(P2, K2)* to end. Turn work.

ROW 12: As row 4 of pattern stitch.

You are now done shaping the neck for the 2-year and 3-year sizes.

• When you are done with the bind-off instructions, compare the length of the front piece to the length of the back. If the front and the back measure the same, bind off the remaining stitches.

SHAPING THE CREW NECK

RIGHT FRONT . . . when number of stitches cast on is NOT divisible by 4 (right side when worn). Begin bind-offs for neck edge on a row 2 of the pattern stitch.

ROW 1: As row 1 of pattern stitch. Turn work.

ROW 2: Bind off 4 stitches. P1 *(K2, P2)* to end. Turn work.

ROW 3: As row 3 of pattern stitch. Turn work.

ROW 4: Bind off 3 stitches. K2 *(P2, K2)* to end. Turn work.

ROW 6: As row 1 of pattern stitch. Turn work.

ROW 7: Bind off 2 stitches. *(K2, P2)* to end. Turn work.

ROW 8: As row 3 of pattern stitch. Turn work.

ROW 9: Bind off 1 stitch. P1, K2 *(P2, K2)* to end. Turn work.

You are now done shaping the neck for the 0–3-month and the 3–6-month sizes.

ROW 10: As row 1 of pattern stitch. Turn work.

ROW 11: Bind off 1 stitch. P2 *(K2, P2)* to end. Turn work.

You are now done shaping the neck for the 1-year size.

ROW 12: As row 3 of the pattern stitch. Turn work.

ROW 13: Bind off 1 stitch. K1, *(P2, K2)* to end.

You are now done shaping the neck for the 2-year and 3-year sizes.

RIGHT FRONT. . . when number of stitches cast on IS divisible by 4. Begin bind-offs for right neck edge on a row 2 of the pattern stitch.

ROW 1: As row 1 of pattern stitch. Turn work.

ROW 2: Bind off 4 stitches. K1, P2 *(K2, P2)* to end. Turn work.

ROW 3: As row 3 of pattern stitch. Turn work.

ROW 4: Bind off 3 stitches. *(P2, K2)* to end. Turn work.

ROW 5: As row 1 of pattern stitch. Turn work.

ROW 6: Bind off 2 stitches. P2 *(K2, P2)* to end. Turn work.

ROW 7: As row 3 of pattern stitch. Turn work.

ROW 8: Bind off 1 stitch. K1 *(P2, K2)* to end. Turn work.

You are now done shaping the neck for the 0–3-month and the 3–6-month sizes.

ROW 9: As row 1 of pattern stitch. Turn work.

ROW 10: Bind off 1 stitch. *(K2, P2)* to end. Turn work.

You are now done shaping the neck for the 1-year size.

ROW 11: As row 3 of the pattern stitch. Turn work.

ROW 12: Bind off 1 stitch. P1, K2 *(P2, K2)* to end. Turn work.

You are now done shaping the neck for the 2-year and 3-year sizes.

• When you are done with the bind-off instructions, compare the length of the front piece to the length of the back. If the front and the back measure the same, bind off the remaining stitches.

WHEN THE NUMBER OF STITCHES CAST ON IS DIVISIBLE BY 4:

ROW 1: K2 *(K2, P2)* to last 2 stitches, K2.

ROW 2: K2 *(K2, P2)* to last 2 stitches, K2.

ROW 3: K2 *(P2, K2)* to last 2 stitches, K2.

ROW 4: K2 *(P2, K2)* to last 2 stitches, K2.

ROW 5: K2, increase as a purl, *(K2, P2)* to last 2 stitches, increase as a knit, K2.

ROW 6: K2, P1 *(K2, P2)* to last 3 stitches, K1, K2.

ROW 7: K2, K1 *(P2, K2)* to last 3 stitches, P1, K2.

ROW 8: K2, K1 *(P2, K2)* to last 3 stitches, P1, K2.

ROW 9: K2, increase as a purl, P1 *(K2, P2) * to last 3 stitches K1, increase as a knit, K2.

ROW 10: K2, P2 *(K2, P2)* to last 4 stitches, K2, K2.

ROW 11: K2, K2 *(P2, K2)* to last 4 stitches, P2, K2.

ROW 12: K2, K2 *(P2, K2)* to last 4 stitches, P2, K2.

ROW 13: K2, increase as a knit, *(K2, P2)* to last 2 stitches, increase as a purl, K2.

ROW 14: K2, P1 *(K2, P2)* to last 3 stitches, K1, K2.

ROW 15: K2, K1 *(P2, K2)* to last 3 stitches, P1, K2.

ROW 16: K2, K1 *(P2, K2)* to last 3 stitches, P1, K2.

ROW 17: K2, increase as a knit l, P1 *(K2, P2)* to last 3 stitches, K1, increase as a purl, K2.

ROW 18: K2, P2 *(K2, P2)* to last 4 stitches, K2, K2.

ROW 19: K2, K2 *(P2, K2)* to last 4 stitches, P2, K2.

ROW 20: K2, K2 *(P2, K2)* to last 4 stitches, P2, K2.

Repeat rows 5–20 until the correct number of increases has been worked.

WHEN THE NUMBER OF STITCHES CAST ON IS NOT DIVISIBLE BY 4:

ROW 1: K2, K2 *(P2, K2)* to last 2 stitches, K2.

ROW 2: K2, P2 *(K2, P2)* to last 2 stitches, K2.

ROW 3: K2, P2 *(K2, P2)* to last 2 stitches, K2.

ROW 4: K2, K2 *(P2, K2)* to last 2 stitches, K2.

ROW 5: K2, increase as a purl, K2 *(P2, K2)* to last 2 stitches, increase as a purl, K2.

ROW 6: K2, K1, P2 *(K2, P2)* to last 3 stitches, K1, K2.

ROW 7: K2, K1, P2 *(K2, P2)* to last 3 stitches, K1, K2.

ROW 8: K2, P1, K2 *(P2, K2)* to last 3 stitches, P1, K2.

ROW 9: K2, increase as a purl, P1 ,K2 *(P2, K2)* to last 3 stitches, P1, increase as a purl, K2.

ROW 10: K2, K2, P2 *(K2, P2)* to last 4 stitches, K2, K2.

ROW 11: K2, K2, P2 *(K2, P2)* to last 4 stitches, K2, K2.

ROW 12: K2 *(P2, K2)* to last 4 stitches P2, K2.

ROW 13: K2, increase as a knit, *(P2, K2)* to last 4 stitches, P2, increase as a knit, K2.

ROW 14: K2, P1 *(K2, P2)* to last 5 stitches, K2, P1, K2.

ROW 15: K2, P1 *(K2, P2)* to last 5 stitches, K2, P1, K2.

ROW 16: K2, K1 *(P2, K2)* to last 5 stitches, P2, K1, K2.

ROW 17: K2, increase as a knit, K1 *P2, K2* to last 5 stitches, P2, K1, increase as a knit, K2.

ROW 18: K2, P2 *(K2, P2)* to last 4 stitches, K2, K2.

ROW 19: K2, P2 *(K2, P2)* to last 2 stitches, K2.

ROW 20: K2, K2 *(P2, K2)* to last 2 stitches, K2.

Repeat rows 5–20 until the correct number of increases has been worked.

NOTE:

To increase as a purl, work the bar method as you would if you were increasing as a knit, but purl the loop instead of knitting it.

to bobble or not to bobble

We like to go shopping at all the fashionable shops in the city in order to get new sweater ideas. On our very first expedition of this sort, we saw a hat and sweater set similar to this one. Julie quickly knit it up, and it has been a favorite among our customers ever since. Both the hat and the sweater are just stockinette stitch—aside from the bobbles, which are simple and fun to make. And if you don't like the bobbles or find them a little too intimidating, the sweater still looks cute with just 8 rows of garter stitch at the bottom. We also prefer the garter-stitch bottom if you are making a boy's version.

BOBBLE STITCH:

Make 5 stitches into 1 stitch by K1 into front, back, front, back, and front of the stitch, *(turn K5, turn P5)* twice, turn, K2tog, K1, K2tog, turn P3tog. (bobble)

NOTE: If you use chenille or a cotton yarn for this pattern, make sure you knit the row before the bobble row loosely.

NOTE: For the boy's version: Work 8 rows of garter stitch before beginning stockinette stitch instead of doing bobbles at the beginning of all pieces.

sweater

BACK:

With #5 needle and color A, cast on 41 (43, 49, 55, 61) stitches. Knit 1 row. Work **Bobble Row** as follows: K5 (3, 3, 3, 3)* (bobble, K5) 5 (6, 7, 8, 9) times, bobble, K5 (3, 3, 3, 3). Knit 1 row. Continue in St st stitch with a knit row in color A until piece measures 5″ (5½″, 6″, 6¾″, 7½″) from the cast-on edge, ending with a WS row. Change to color B. Continue to work in St st until piece measures 10″ (11″, 12″, 13½″, 15″) from cast-on edge, ending with a WS row. Bind off all stitches loosely.

LEFT FRONT:

With #5 needle and color A, cast on 21 (21, 25, 27, 31) stitches. Knit 1 row. Work **Bobble Row** as follows: K4 (4, 3, 4, 3), (bobble, K5) 2 (2, 3, 3, 4) times, bobble, K4 (4, 3, 4, 3). Knit 1 row. Continue in St st beginning with a knit row until piece measures 5″ (5½″, 6″, 6¾″, 7½″) from bottom. Change to color B. Continue to work in St st until piece measures 8″ (9″, 9½″, 11″, 12½″) from cast-on edge, ending with a RS row. **Shape Crew Neck:** At beginning of neck edge, every other row, bind off 0 (0, 4, 4, 4) stitches once, 3 stitches once, 2 stitches once, 1 stitch 3 (3, 1, 2, 2) times. (See step-by-step instructions.) Continue to work in St st on remaining 13 (13, 15, 16, 20) stitches until piece measures 10″ (11″, 12″, 13½″, 15″) from cast-on edge, ending with a WS row. Bind off all stitches loosely.

RIGHT FRONT:

Work as for left front, reversing shaping, but cast on with color B and change to color A at 5″ (5½″, 6″, 6¾″, 7½″).

SLEEVES:

(1 in color A and one in color B)

With #5 needle, cast on 25 (27, 29, 31, 31) stitches. Knit 1 row. **Bobble Row:** K3 (4, 2, 3, 3)* (bobble, K5) 3 (3, 4, 4, 4) times. Knit 1 row. Continue in St st beginning with a knit row. **AT THE SAME TIME,** increase 1 stitch at each end of every 4th row 9 (9, 10, 11, 12) times until you have 43 (45, 49, 53, 55) stitches.

NOTE: INCREASE LEAVING 2 EDGE STITCHES ON EITHER SIDE OF WORK. THIS MEANS YOU SHOULD KNIT 2 STITCHES, INCREASE 1 STITCH, KNIT TO THE LAST 2 STITCHES, INCREASE 1 STITCH, THEN KNIT THE 2 REMAINING STITCHES. INCREASING LIKE THIS MAKES IT EASIER TO SEW UP YOUR SEAMS.

YARN: CRYSTAL PALACE YARNS, CHENILLE (98 YARDS / 50G BALL)

FIBER CONTENT: 100% COTTON

COLORS:
BOY VERSION: 5800 AND 4021
GIRL VERSION: 2230 AND 8211

AMOUNT: 2 (2, 2, 3, 3) BALLS OF EACH COLOR

TOTAL YARDAGE: 392 (392, 588, 784, 784) YARDS

GAUGE: 4 STITCHES = 1 INCH; 16 STITCHES = 4 INCHES

NEEDLE SIZE: US #5 (3.75MM) OR SIZE NEEDED TO OBTAIN GAUGE

SIZES: 0–3 MONTHS (3–6 MONTHS, 1 YEAR, 2 YEAR, 3 YEAR)

KNITTED MEASUREMENTS: SWEATER: WIDTH = 10″ (10″, 12″, 13½″, 15″), LENGTH = 10″ (11″, 12″, 13½″, 15″), SLEEVE LENGTH = 6″ (6½″, 7″, 8″, 10″) HAT CIRCUMFERENCE: 14″ (14¾″, 15½″, 16″, 17″)

OTHER MATERIALS: 5 BUTTONS

Continue in St st until piece measures 6″ (6½″, 7″, 8″, 10″) from cast-on edge, ending with a WS row. Bind off all stitches loosely.

FINISHING:

Sew shoulder seams together. Sew sleeves on. Sew up side and sleeve seams.

For girl version, pick up button bands first, then pick up neckband. For boy version, pick up neckband first.

GIRL VERSION: Buttonholes should be placed on the right front as the sweater is worn.

Button band: With the color of your choice, #5 needles, and the RS facing, pick up 54 (58, 62, 66, 70) stitches. Work 5 rows in knit, then bind off loosely.

Buttonhole band: Pick up as for button band. Knit 2 rows. **Buttonhole row:** K2 (2, 2, 2, 2) *YO loosely around needle, K2tog, knit 7 (8, 8, 9, 10)* 4 times, end K2tog, YO, K2 (2, 2, 2, 2). Next row: Knit. Then work 2 more rows in garter stitch and bind off.

Neckband: With RS facing, #5 needle, and the color of your choice, beginning at middle of right buttonhole side, pick up 43 (45, 51, 57, 57) stitches around neck. Work in garter stitch for 3″ ending with RS row. **Bobble Row:** K3 (4, 4, 4, 4), *(bobble, K5)* 6 (6, 7, 8, 8) times, bobble, K3 (4, 4, 4, 4). Knit 2 more rows. Bind off all stitches loosely.

BOY VERSION: Buttonholes should be placed on the left front as the sweater is worn.

Neckband: With RS facing, #5 needles, and the color of your choice, pick up 40 (42, 48, 54, 54) stitches around neck. Work in garter stitch for 1″. Bind off all stitches loosely.

Button band: With the color of your choice, #5 needles, and the RS facing, pick up 58 (62, 66, 70, 74) stitches. Work 5 rows in knit, then bind off loosely.

Buttonhole band: Pick up as for button band side. Knit 2 rows. **Buttonhole row:** K2 (2, 2, 2, 2) *YO loosely around needle, K2tog, knit 11 (12, 13, 14, 15)* 4 times, end K2tog, YO, K2 (2, 2, 2, 2). Next row: Knit. Then work 2 more rows in garter stitch and bind off.

h a t

With #5 needle and color A, cast on 57 (59, 63, 65, 69) stitches. Work in garter stitch for 3 rows (if you are not doing bobbles, work in garter stitch for 6 rows and then change to color B and begin St st). Work bobble row as follows: K4 (2, 4, 2, 4), *(bobble, K5)* 8 (9, 9, 10, 10) times, bobble, K4 (2, 4, 2, 4). Work 2 more rows in knit. Beginning with a knit row, work in St st for 1″. Change to color B and continue in St st until hat measures 5″ (5½″, 5¾″, 6″, 6″) from cast-on edge. Change back to color A and work decreases as follows:

ROW 1: *(K5 stitches, K2tog)* across row. Turn work.

ROWS 2, 4, 6, 8, AND 10: Purl 1 row. Turn work.

ROW 3: *(K4 stitches, K2tog)* across row. Turn work.

ROW 5: *(K3 stitches, K2tog)* across row. Turn work.

ROW 7: *(K2 stitches, K2tog)* across row. Turn work.

ROW 9: *(K1 stitch, K2tog)* across row. Turn work.

ROW 11: *(K2tog)* across row.

Cut yarn, leaving approximately 20″. With a yarn needle, thread yarn through remaining loops and sew down seam. For hat with bobbles, fold up the bottom of the hat and lightly tack it down.

LEFT FRONT
(left side when worn)

For 1-year, 2-year, and 3-year sizes, begin with row 1. For all other sizes, begin with row 3.

ROW 1: Bind off 4 stitches. Purl to end. Turn work.

ROW 2: Knit. Turn work.

ROW 3: Bind off 3 stitches. Purl to end. Turn work.

ROW 4: Knit. Turn work.

ROW 5: Bind off 2 stitches. Purl to end. Turn work.

ROW 6: Knit. Turn work.

ROW 7: Bind off 1 stitch. Purl to end. Turn work.

ROW 8: Knit. Turn work.

Repeat rows 7 and 8 2 (2, 0, 1, 1) more times.

RIGHT FRONT
(right side when worn)

For 1-year, 2-year, and 3-year sizes, begin with row 1. For all other sizes, begin with row 3.

ROW 1: Bind off 4 stitches. Knit to end. Turn work.

ROW 2: Purl. Turn work.

ROW 3: Bind off 3 stitches. Knit to end. Turn work.

ROW 4: Purl. Turn work.

ROW 5: Bind off 2 stitches. Knit to end. Turn work.

ROW 6: Purl. Turn work.

ROW 7: Bind off 1 stitch. Knit to end. Turn work.

ROW 8: Purl. Turn work.

Repeat rows 7 and 8 2 (2, 0, 1, 1) more times.

• When you are done with the bind-off instructions, compare the length of the front piece to the length of the back. If the front and the back measure the same, bind off the remaining stitches.

to bobble or not to bobble, for him

v-neck pullovers

V-neck pullovers are a classic design. They are knit like crew-neck pullovers, except the neck is shaped like a *V*. We kept these patterns as simple as possible—all in stockinette stitch. But you can certainly use the basic shape and add stripes or try another stitch for your own personal touch. If you haven't already, you will perfect making two common decreases, knit 2 together **(K2tog)** and slip slip knit **(ssk)** by the time you are done with the sweater. *Mikey Liked It* is a V-neck with rolled edges. It is especially simple because no finishing is required around the neck. *The Prepster* is almost the same, but we added ribbings at all edges.

mikey liked it

Mikey had knit a million scarves, baby and adult hats, and baby blankets. But the idea of a sweater intimidated her. She just wasn't sure she would like it. Finally, we convinced her that baby sweaters were easy and it was time she learned some new techniques. We assured her that if she tried it, she would like it. So she decided to make a V-neck pullover for her friend Yvonne's son, Kai Noah. We kept the pattern as simple as possible, with roll edges on the sleeves and the bottom, and the V-neck designed so she didn't have to pick up stitches. Mikey learned how to increase while making sleeves and decrease while shaping the V-neck. The sweater turned out great, and she was happy we made her try something new because in the end she liked it.

BACK:

With #9 needle and 1 strand of each color, cast on 40 (44, 48, 54, 60) stitches. Work in St st until piece measures 10" (11", 12", 13½", 15") from cast-on edge, ending with a WS row. Bind off all stitches loosely.

FRONT:

Work as for back until piece measures 5½" (6", 7", 8½", 10") from cast-on edge, ending with a WS row. **Shape V-Neck:** Place a marker at the center. Row 1: Knit until 4 stitches before the marker, K2tog, K2. Turn work around as though you were at the end of the row. You are going to ignore the rest of the stitches. Row 2: Purl. Row 3: Knit. Row 4: Purl. Repeat rows 1–4 2 (4, 4, 3, 2) more times, then repeat rows 1 and 2 7 (5, 5, 7, 9) times until you have 10 (12, 14, 16, 18) stitches. (See step-by-step instructions.) Continue to work on these stitches until piece measures 10" (11", 12", 13½", 15") from cast-on edge, ending with a WS row. Bind off remaining stitches loosely. Attach yarn to other side. You should be on a knit row. Row 1: K2, SSK, knit until end. Row 2: Purl back.

Row 3: Knit. Row 4: Purl. Repeat rows 1–4 2 (4, 4, 3, 2) more times, then repeat rows 1 and 2 7 (5, 5, 7, 9) times until you have 10 (12, 14, 16, 18) stitches. (See step-by-step instructions.) Continue to work on these stitches until piece measures 10" (11", 12", 13½", 15") from cast-on edge, ending with a WS row. Bind off remaining stitches loosely.

SLEEVES:

With #9 needle, cast on 24 (26, 26, 28, 30) stitches. Work in St st. **AT THE SAME TIME,** increase 1 stitch at each edge every 4th row 8 (8, 9, 9, 10) times until you have 40 (42, 44, 46, 50) stitches.

NOTE: INCREASE LEAVING 2 EDGE STITCHES ON EITHER SIDE OF WORK. THIS MEANS YOU SHOULD KNIT 2 STITCHES, INCREASE 1 STITCH, KNIT TO THE LAST 2 STITCHES, INCREASE 1 STITCH, AND THEN KNIT THE REMAINING 2 STITCHES. INCREASING LIKE THIS MAKES IT EASIER TO SEW UP YOUR SEAMS.

Continue in St st until sleeve measures 6" (6½", 7", 8", 10") from cast-on edge, ending with a WS row. Bind off all stitches loosely.

FINISHING:

Sew shoulder seams together. Sew on sleeves, then sew up side and sleeve seams.

YARN: BLUE SKY ALPACA (120 YARDS / 50G BALL)

FIBER CONTENT: 100% ALPACA

COLORS:
GIRL VERSION: 50 AND 512
BOY VERSION: 403 AND 05

AMOUNT: 3 (3, 3, 4, 4) BALLS OF EACH COLOR

TOTAL YARDAGE: 720 (720, 720, 960, 960) YARDS

GAUGE: 4 STITCHES = 1 INCH; 16 STITCHES = 4 INCHES

NEEDLE SIZE: US #9 (5.5MM) OR SIZE NEEDED TO OBTAIN GAUGE

SIZES: 0–3 MONTHS (3–6 MONTHS, 1 YEAR, 2 YEAR, 3 YEAR)

KNITTED MEASUREMENTS: WIDTH = 10" (11", 12", 13½", 15"), LENGTH = 10" (11", 12", 13½", 15"), SLEEVE LENGTH = 6" (6½", 7", 8", 10")

Yarn is worked double throughout the sweater—this means you should hold 1 strand of each color, and work them together as though they are 1.

mikey liked it, for her

STEP-BY-STEP GUIDE TO SHAPING THE V-NECK

First you must place a marker around the needle in the center of the work.

ROW 1: Knit to 4 stitches before the marker, K2tog, K2. Turn work.

ROW 2: Purl. Turn work.

ROW 3: Knit. Turn work.

ROW 4: Purl. Turn work.

Repeat rows 1–4 2 (4, 4, 3, 2) more times. Then repeat rows 1 and 2 7 (5, 5, 7, 9) more times.

Attach yarn to the other side of the *V*.

ROW 1: K2, SSK, knit to the end of the row. Turn work.

ROW 2: Purl. Turn work.

ROW 3: Knit. Turn work.

ROW 4: Purl. Turn work.

Repeat rows 1–4 2 (4, 4, 3, 2) more times. Then repeat rows 1 and 2 7 (5, 5, 7, 9) more times.

• When you are done with the decrease instructions, compare the length of the front piece to the length of the back. If the front and back measure the same, bind off the remaining stitches. If the front is too short, continue knitting and purling until the pieces are of equal length, then bind off.

the prepster

Kim wanted to make a sweater for her friend's newborn son.
Her friend, she said, was still living in the preppy years. So Kim
wanted to knit a preppy sweater but add a bit of her own
style. Well, you can't get much preppier than a V-
neck pullover. Kim also wanted to add stripes in
three or four colors. However, the problem was
that she was going to be traveling on a plane
with her young daughter and wanted to make
things as simple as possible. She
didn't want to keep changing balls of yarn. Luckily
we had this yarn that
stripes itself. And with
such great yarn, we
could not resist making
a hat too. Her friend
loved the sweater
even without the little
Izod alligator.

sweater

BACK:

With #6 needle, cast on 44 (50, 54, 62, 68) stitches. Work in K1, P1 ribbing for 6 rows. Change to #8 needle and work in St st until piece measures 10" (11", 12", 13½", 15") from cast-on edge, ending with a WS row. Bind off all stitches loosely.

FRONT:

Work as for back until piece measures 5" (6", 7", 8½", 10") from cast-on edge, ending with a WS row. **Shape V-Neck:** Place a marker at the center. Row 1: Knit until 4 stitches before the marker, K2tog, K2. Turn work around as though you were at the end of the row. You are going to ignore the rest of the stitches. Row 2: Purl. Row 3: Knit. Row 4: Purl. Repeat rows 1–4 6 (5, 4, 2, 1) more times, then repeat rows 1 and 2 2 (4, 5, 10, 12) times until you have 13 (15, 17, 18, 20) stitches. (See step-by-step instructions.) Continue to work on these stitches until piece measures 10" (11", 12", 13½" 15") from cast-on edge, ending with a WS row. Bind off remaining stitches loosely. Attach yarn to other side. You should be on a knit row. Row 1: K2, SSK, knit until end. Row 2: Purl back. Row 3: Knit. Row 4:

Purl. Repeat rows 1–4 6 (5, 4, 2, 1) more times, then repeat rows 1 and 2 2 (4, 5, 10, 12) times until you have 13 (15, 17, 18, 20) stitches. (See step-by-step instructions.) Continue to work on these stitches until piece measures 10" (11", 12", 13½", 15") from cast-on edge, ending with a WS row. Bind off remaining stitches.

SLEEVES:

With #6 needle, cast on 28 (30, 32, 34, 36) stitches. Work in K1, P1 ribbing as for back. Change to #8 needles. Work in St st. **AT THE SAME TIME,** increase 1 stitch at each edge every 4th row 8 (8, 9, 10, 11) times until you have 44 (46, 50, 54, 58) stitches.

NOTE: INCREASE LEAVING 2 EDGE STITCHES ON EITHER SIDE OF WORK. THIS MEANS YOU SHOULD KNIT 2 STITCHES, INCREASE 1 STITCH, KNIT TO THE LAST 2 STITCHES, INCREASE 1 STITCH, AND THEN KNIT THE REMAINING 2 STITCHES. INCREASING LIKE THIS MAKES IT EASIER TO SEW UP YOUR SEAMS.

Continue in St st until sleeve measures 6" (6½", 7", 8", 10") from cast-on edge, ending with a WS row. Bind off all stitches loosely.

YARN: NORO, KUREYON (108 YARDS / 50G BALL)

FIBER CONTENT: 100% WOOL

COLORS:
GIRL VERSION: 102
BOY VERSION: 52

AMOUNT: 3 (4, 4, 5, 5) BALLS

TOTAL YARDAGE: 324 (432, 432, 540, 540) YARDS

GAUGE: 4½ STITCHES = 1 INCH; 18 STITCHES = 4 INCHES

NEEDLE SIZE: US #8 (5MM) FOR BODY OR SIZE NEEDED TO OBTAIN GAUGE; US #6 (4MM) FOR RIBBING; CIRCULAR 16" US #6 (4MM) FOR RIBBING AROUND NECK

SIZES: 0–3 MONTHS (3–6 MONTHS, 1 YEAR, 2 YEAR, 3 YEAR)

KNITTED MEASUREMENTS: SWEATER: WIDTH = 10" (11", 12", 13½", 15"), LENGTH = 10" (11", 12", 13½", 15"), SLEEVE LENGTH = 6" (6½", 7", 8", 10") HAT CIRCUMFERENCE: 14" (14¾", 15½", 16", 17")

NOTE: This yarn stripes as it knits. Each ball has the same order of colors, but the balls will start at a different point. If you use this yarn and want the colors to match up, you need to wind the balls to start at the same color.

FINISHING:

Sew shoulder seams together. Sew on sleeves and then sew up side and sleeve seams. With a circular 16" #6 needle and RS of right back neck facing, pick up 20 (26, 28, 30, 32) stitches across back neck, 28 down left front, place marker, 1 in center, place marker, 28 up right front. Work as follows: K1, P1 rib until 2 stitches before first marker, SSK, slip marker, knit 1 stitch, slip marker, K2tog, continue in K1, P1 rib stitch to right back neck. Work 4 more rounds in this manner, then bind off all stitches loosely.

STEP-BY-STEP GUIDE TO SHAPING THE V-NECK

First you must place a marker around the needle in the center of the work.

ROW 1: Knit to 4 stitches before the marker, K2tog, K2. Turn work.

ROW 2: Purl. Turn work.

ROW 3: Knit. Turn work.

ROW 4: Purl. Turn work.

Repeat rows 1–4 6 (5, 4, 2, 1) more times. Then repeat rows 1 and 2 2 (4, 5, 10, 12) more times.

At the center of the sweater, attach yarn to the other side of the V.

ROW 1: K2, SSK, knit to the end of the row. Turn work.

ROW 2: Purl. Turn work.

ROW 3: Knit. Turn work.

ROW 4: Purl. Turn work.

Repeat rows 1–4 6 (5, 4, 2, 1) more times. Then repeat rows 1 and 2 2 (4, 5, 10, 12) more times.

• When you are done with the decrease instructions, compare the length of the front piece to the length of the back. If the front and back measure the same, bind off the remaining stitches. If the front is too short, continue knitting and purling until the pieces are of equal length, then bind off.

• If you are using a self-striping yarn, when you start shaping your V-neck you may want to wind through a second ball of yarn to find the same color point before attaching it to the second side.

hat

With #8 needle, cast on 64 (66, 70, 72, 76) stitches. Work in St st until piece measures 5″ (5½″, 5¾″, 6″, 6″) from cast-on edge, ending with a WS row. Work decreases as follows:

ROW 1: *(K5 stitches, K2tog)* across row. Turn work.

ROWS 2, 4, 6, 8, AND 10: Purl. Turn work.

ROW 3: *(K4 stitches, K2tog)* across row. Turn work.

ROW 5: *(K3 stitches, K2tog)* across row. Turn work.

ROW 7: *(K2 stitches, K2tog)* across row. Turn work.

ROW 9: *(K1 stitch, K2tog)* across row. Turn work.

ROW 11: *(K2tog)* across row.

Cut yarn, leaving approximately 20″. With a yarn needle, thread through remaining loops and sew down seam.

the prepster, for her

We added this chapter for those who prefer V-neck cardigans to crew-neck cardigans. We chose two designs that differ by their edgings and the use of color. *Cleo's Cardigan*, named for the cute redhead for whom this sweater was designed, is knit in a stripe pattern with a bit of fuzz. Cleo gets stopped in the streets and receives rave reviews whenever she wears it. We also knit this sweater in different colors without the technohair, and it became a great sweater for a little guy too. *Mary, Mary . . . Whatcha Knitting* is a store favorite. It is knit in stockinette with a garter ridge in the center and is edged with single crochet. Choosing colors for either is a way to show your originality.

v-neck
cardigans

Cleo's Colors

Jordana's niece Cleo was five years old when she came into our shop and announced that she wanted Jordana to knit her a sweater. At the time, Cleo was a self-proclaimed girly girl who only wore skirts and dresses and whose favorite colors were pink, red, and purple. She loved all things frilly or fussy. Jordana showed Cleo various sweater options, but the strong-minded Cleo rejected them all. Cleo then set about looking around the store choosing her own yarns and colors. She chose the red and pink cotton classic and the red fuzzy technohair. So Jordana made her a striped sweater in the colors pictured on the next page. Take away the fuzzy yarn and it's a great pattern for a boy too.

PATTERN STITCH:

4 rows St st in color B

2 rows garter in color C

4 rows St st in color B

6 rows St st in color A

BACK:

With #4 needle and color A, cast on 50 (54, 60, 68, 76) stitches. Work in K1, P1 ribbing for 6 rows. Change to #6 needle and work in stripe pattern until piece measures 10″ (11″, 12″, 13½″, 15″) from cast-on edge, ending with a WS row. Bind off all stitches loosely.

FRONT: (make 2, reverse shaping)

With #4 needle and color A, cast on 24 (26, 30, 34, 38) stitches. Work in K1, P1 ribbing for 6 rows. Change to #6 needle and work in pattern stitch until piece measures 6″ (7″, 8½″, 9″, 9½″) from cast-on edge, ending on a WS row. **Shape V-Neck:** For left front when worn: Row 1: Knit until last 4 stitches, K2tog, K2. Row 2: Purl. Row 3: Knit. Row 4: Purl. Repeat rows 1–4 5 (5, 5, 4, 7) more times. Then repeat rows 1 and 2 4 (4, 5, 7, 5) times. (See step-by-step instructions.) Continue to work on remaining 14 (16, 19, 22, 25) stitches until piece measures 10″ (11″, 12″, 13½″, 15″) from cast-on edge, ending with a WS row. Bind off all stitches loosely. For right side: Row 1: K2, SSK, knit to end. Row 2: Purl. Row 3: Knit. Row 4: Purl. Repeat rows 1–4 5 (5, 5, 4, 7) more times. Then repeat rows 1 and 2 4 (4, 5, 7, 5) times. (See step-by-step instructions.) Continue to work on remaining 14 (16, 19, 22, 25) stitches until piece measures 10″ (11″, 12″, 13½″, 15″) from cast-on edge, ending with a WS row. Bind off all stitches loosely.

YARN: TAHKI, COTTON CLASSIC (108 YARDS / 50G BALL); GEDIFRA, TECHNOHAIR (99 YARDS / 50G BALL)

FIBER CONTENT: 100% MERCERIZED COTTON; TECHNOHAIR: 100% POLYAMIDE

COLORS:
GIRL VERSION: A-3997 (RED), B-3458 (PINK), C-9644 (TECHNOHAIR)
BOY VERSION A-3725 (GREEN), B-3039 (GRAY), C-3003 (OFF-WHITE)

AMOUNT: 2 (2, 3, 3, 3) BALLS COLOR A; 2 (2, 3, 3, 3) BALLS COLOR B; 1 (1, 1, 1, 1) BALL COLOR C

TOTAL YARDAGE: 532 (532, 748, 748, 748) YARDS

GAUGE: 5 STITCHES = 1 INCH; 20 STITCHES = 4 INCHES

NEEDLE SIZE: US #6 (4MM) FOR BODY OR SIZE NEEDED TO OBTAIN GAUGE; US #4 (3.5MM) FOR RIBBING

SIZES: 0–3 MONTHS (3–6 MONTHS, 1 YEAR, 2 YEAR, 3 YEAR)

KNITTED MEASUREMENTS: WIDTH = 10″ (11″, 12″, 13½″, 15″), LENGTH =10″ (11″, 12″, 13½″, 15″), SLEEVE LENGTH = 6″ (6½″, 7″, 8″, 10″)

OTHER MATERIALS: 3 BUTTONS

cleo's colors for her

SLEEVES:

With #4 needle and color A, cast on 30 (32, 34, 36, 38) stitches. Work in K1, P1 ribbing for 6 rows. Change to #6 needle and work in pattern stitch. **AT THE SAME TIME,** increase 1 stitch at each edge every 4th row 9 (10, 11, 13, 16) times until you have 48 (52, 56, 62, 70) stitches.

NOTE: INCREASE LEAVING 2 EDGE STITCHES ON EITHER SIDE OF WORK. THIS MEANS YOU SHOULD KNIT 2 STITCHES, INCREASE 1 STITCH, KNIT TO THE LAST 2 STITCHES, INCREASE 1 STITCH, AND THEN KNIT THE REMAINING 2 STITCHES. INCREASING LIKE THIS MAKES IT EASIER TO SEW UP YOUR SEAMS.

Continue in pattern stitch until piece measures 6″ (6½″, 7″, 8″, 10″) from cast-on edge, ending with a WS row. Bind off all stitches loosely.

FINISHING:

Sew shoulder seams together. Sew sleeves to body. Sew up side and sleeve seams. With a #4 needle, color A, and RS facing of right front, pick up 36 (42, 42, 50, 52) stitches up right front, place marker, pick up 24 (24, 30, 30, 36) stitches from right V, place marker, pick up 22 (22, 22, 24, 26) stitches across back neck edge, place marker, pick up 24 (24, 30, 30, 36) stitches down left V, place marker, pick up 36 (42, 42, 50, 52) down left front. Work in K1, P1 ribbing for 2 rows. **For boys:** Rib 2 (2, 2, 2, 3), *YO, Rib 2tog, Rib 13 (16, 16, 20, 21) stitches* 2 times, K2tog, YO, Rib 2 (2, 2, 2, 3). Continue in established rib until end of row. Work 2 more rows. Bind off all stitches loosely. **For girls:** Work as for boys but place buttonholes after you reach 4th marker.

STEP-BY-STEP GUIDE TO SHAPING THE V-NECK

Remember to continue to work in the stripe pattern. If necessary cut the colors instead of carrying them.

LEFT FRONT
(left side when worn)

ROW 1: Knit to last 4 stitches, K2tog, K2. Turn work.

ROW 2: Purl. Turn work.

ROW 3: Knit. Turn work.

ROW 4: Purl. Turn work.

Repeat rows 1–4 5 (5, 5, 4, 7) more times. Then repeat rows 1 and 2 4 (4, 5, 7, 5) more times.

RIGHT FRONT
(right side when worn)

ROW 1: K2, SSK, knit to the end of the row. Turn work.

ROW 2: Purl. Turn work.

ROW 3: Knit. Turn work.

ROW 4: Purl. Turn work.

Repeat rows 1–4 5 (5, 5, 4, 7) more times. Then repeat rows 1 and 2 4 (4, 5, 7, 5) more times.

• When you are done with the decrease instructions, compare the length of the front piece to the length of the back. If the front and back measure the same, bind off the remaining stitches. If the front is too short, continue knitting and purling until the pieces are of equal length, then bind off.

mary, mary... whatcha knitting?

With two sons, a daughter, and a full-time job, Mary doesn't have a lot of time to knit. In fact, most of her knitting is done on the go—in the car, on the bus, or in the air. She likes quick, easy, portable projects she can make for Nathaniel, Jacob, and Jessica. Jessica, however, is a headstrong three-year-old who has very specific likes and dislikes when it comes to colors. To prevent a disaster, Mary brought her to the store to pick out yarn and colors for the sweater she would make her. She liked pinks and yellow. We designed this sweater just for her, and her brothers liked it so much Mary decided to make one for each of them too. Mary had a lot of knitting to do!

BACK:

With #7 needle and color A, cast on 44 (50, 54, 60, 68) stitches. Work in St st until piece measures 5" (5½", 6", 7", 8") from cast-on edge, ending with a WS row. Change to color B and work 2 rows of knit. Change to color C and work in St st until piece measures 10" (11", 12", 13½", 15") from cast-on edge, ending with a WS row. Bind off all stitches loosely.

FRONT: (make 2, reverse shaping)

With #7 needle and color A, cast on 22 (25, 27, 30, 34) stitches. Work in St st until piece measures 5" (5½", 6", 7", 8") from cast-on edge, ending with a WS row. Change to color B and work 2 rows of knit. Change to color C and work in St st until piece measures 6" (7", 7", 8½", 9½") from cast-on edge, ending with a WS row. **Shape V-Neck:** *For left front (when worn):* Row 1: Knit to last 4 stitches, K2tog, K2. Row 2: Purl. Row 3: Knit. Row 4: Purl. Repeat rows 1–4 1 (1, 4, 4, 5) more time(s). Then repeat rows 1 and 2 8 (8, 5, 6, 6) times until you have 12 (15, 17, 19, 22) stitches. (See step-by-step instructions.) When piece measures 10" (11",

12", 13½", 15") from cast-on edge, ending with a WS row, bind off remaining stitches loosely. *For right front (when worn):* Row 1: K2, SSK, knit to end. Row 2: Purl. Row 3: Knit. Row 4: Purl. Repeat rows 1–4 1 (1, 4, 4, 5) more time(s). Then repeat rows 1 and 2 8 (8, 5, 6, 6) times until you have 12 (15, 17, 19, 22) stitches. (See step-by-step instructions.) When piece measures 10" (11", 12", 13½", 15") from cast-on edge, ending with a WS row, bind off remaining stitches loosely.

SLEEVES:

With #7 needle and color A, cast on 26 (28, 30, 32, 34) stitches. Work in St st. **AT THE SAME TIME,** increase 1 stitch at each edge every 4th row 9 (9, 10, 11, 14) times until you have 44 (46, 50, 54, 62) stitches.

NOTE: INCREASE LEAVING 2 EDGE STITCHES ON EITHER SIDE OF WORK. THIS MEANS YOU SHOULD KNIT 2 STITCHES, INCREASE 1 STITCH, KNIT TO THE LAST 2 STITCHES, INCREASE 1 STITCH, AND THEN KNIT THE REMAINING 2 STITCHES. INCREASING LIKE THIS MAKES IT EASIER TO SEW UP YOUR SEAMS.

YARN: MISSION FALLS 1824 COTTON (84 YARDS / 50G BALL)

FIBER CONTENT: 100% COTTON

COLORS:
GIRL VERSION: A-208, B-209, C-206
BOY VERSION: A-404, B-102, C-202

AMOUNT: 2 (2, 2, 2, 3) BALLS COLOR A; 1 (1, 1, 1, 1) BALL COLOR B; 2 (2, 2, 3, 3) BALLS COLOR C.

TOTAL YARDAGE: 420 (420, 420, 504, 588)

GAUGE: 4½ STITCHES = 1 INCH; 18 STITCHES = 4 INCHES

NEEDLE SIZE: US #7 (4.5MM) OR SIZE NEEDED TO OBTAIN GAUGE; G CROCHET HOOK

SIZES: 0-3 MONTHS (3-6 MONTHS, 1 YEAR, 2 YEAR, 3 YEAR)

KNITTED MEASUREMENTS: WIDTH = 9¾" (11", 12", 13½", 15"), LENGTH =10" (11", 12", 13½", 15"), SLEEVE LENGTH = 6" (6½", 7", 8", 10")

OTHER MATERIALS: 5 BUTTONS FOR GIRL VERSION; 3 BUTTONS FOR BOY VERSION

When piece measures 2½" (2½", 3", 3½", 4") from cast-on edge, ending with a WS row, change to color B and work 2 rows in knit. Change to color C and work in St st until piece measures 6" (6½", 7", 8", 10") from cast-on edge, ending with a WS row. Bind off all stitches loosely.

FINISHING:

Sew shoulder seams together. Sew sleeves on. Sew up side and sleeve seams. Sew sleeves to body so they attach at color B. With a G crochet hook, work 1 row of single crochet in color B around all edges. Place button loops evenly on desired side for buttonholes (5 on the right side for girls, 3 on the left side for boys; this is as the sweater is worn, not as you knit).

STEP-BY-STEP GUIDE TO SHAPING THE V-NECK

LEFT FRONT
(left side when worn)

ROW 1: Knit to last 4 stitches, K2tog, K2. Turn work.

ROW 2: Purl. Turn work.

ROW 3: Knit. Turn work.

ROW 4: Purl. Turn work.

Repeat rows 1–4 1 (1, 4, 4, 5) more time(s). Then repeat rows 1 and 2 8 (8, 5, 6, 6) more times.

RIGHT FRONT
(right side when worn)

ROW 1: K2, SSK, knit to the end of the row. Turn work.

ROW 2: Purl. Turn work.

ROW 3: Knit. Turn work.

ROW 4: Purl. Turn work.

Repeat rows 1–4 1 (1, 4, 4, 5) more time(s). Then repeat rows 1 and 2 8 (8, 5, 6, 6) more times.

• When you are done with the decrease instructions, compare the length of the front piece to the length of the back. If the front and back measure the same, bind off the remaining stitches. If the front is too short, continue knitting and purling until the pieces are of equal length, then bind off.

hats

Knitting a hat is so gratifying. Hats knit up quickly, and they look adorable. They are also a perfect gift, especially if you are short on time but want to give something handmade. The *Jester Hat* is the most whimsical of the bunch we designed. Not to mention it is rather original—not too many kids will be walking around with one. The pattern is a bit more advanced, but people who like to do more than knit and purl will enjoy it because there is a bit of shaping. Choosing colors to complement the pattern is almost as fun as knitting it. *Baby It's You* has color and texture thrown in. We striped three colors in a stockinette and garter-ridge pattern. This is one of those projects that look harder than they are. *Sugar and Spice* is the perfect project for those who want to learn intarsia. At the same time, it stays simple because there is no shaping.

jester hat

This hat is for those of you with a sense of humor. It looks a bit wacky, but little kids look *precious* in floppy, funny hats. Take Susan, for example. Her daughter Devon is a big ham. She has a big, round smiley face with two cute teeth sticking out in front, and she loves to make everybody laugh. Susan wanted to make a hat for Devon that expressed her spunky personality. She wanted it to be colorful, funky, and just downright fun. We thought this jester design fit the bill perfectly. Susan picked four great colors, and the best part was that she had enough yarn left over to make another hat in a different combination of the same colors for her other daughter, Sela.

YARN: FILATURA DI CROSA, ZARA (137 YARDS / 50G BALL)

FIBER CONTENT: 100% MERINO WOOL

COLORS:
GIRL VERSION: A-1503 (PEA), B-1667 (RED), C-6053 (PURPLE), D-1701 (GOLD)
BOY VERSION: A-1494 (LIGHT GRAY), B-1404 (BLACK), C-1468 (MEDIUM GRAY), D-1469 (CHARCOAL)

AMOUNT: 1 BALL EACH COLOR, A, B, C, AND D

TOTAL YARDAGE: 548 YARDS

GAUGE: 5 STITCHES = 1 INCH; 20 STITCHES = 4 INCHES

NEEDLE SIZE: 16″ CIRCULAR US #7 (4.5MM) OR SIZE NEEDED TO OBTAIN GAUGE

SIZES: 0–3 MONTHS (3–6 MONTHS, 1 YEAR, 2 YEAR, 3 YEAR)

KNITTED MEASUREMENTS:
CIRCUMFERENCE: 14″ (14¾″, 15½″, 16″, 17″)

With a #7 16″ circular needle and color A, cast on 70 (74, 76, 80, 86) stitches. Place a marker at the beginning of your row and join stitches in a circle. Make sure all stitches are facing the same way and that you are not twisting them. Work in St st (knitting each round) for 12 rounds. Change to color B and continue in St st until work measures 5″ (5½″, 6″, 6½″, 6½″) from the cast-on edge. Knit 35 (37, 38, 40, 43) stitches and place remaining 35 (37, 38, 40, 43) stitches on a holder. Continue to work in St st on these 35 (37, 38, 40, 43) stitches, back and forth now (knitting 1 row and purling 1 row), while decreasing 1 stitch at each edge of every knit row until 1 stitch remains.

To Decrease: K2, K2tog until 4 stitches remain, K2tog, K2. Cut yarn and pull it through the remaining loop to secure. Place the 35 (37, 38, 40, 43) stitches from the holder back onto the needle, attach color B, and work as for the other side, decreasing 1 stitch at each edge of every knit row until 1 stitch remains. Cut yarn and pull it through the remaining loop to secure.

FINISHING:

Sew up seam on each half.

Make 2 pom-poms, 1 in color C and 1 in color D. Attach 1 pom-pom to the top of each point.

jester hat, for him

baby it's you

YARN: FILATURA DI CROSA, ZARA (137 YARDS / 50G BALL)

FIBER CONTENT: 100% MERINO WOOL

COLORS:
GIRL VERSION: A-1501 (HOT PINK), B-1510 (LIGHT PINK), C-1665 (MEDIUM PINK)
BOY VERSION: A-1663 (DARK BROWN), B-1451 (BONE), C-1476 (MEDIUM BROWN)

AMOUNT: 1 BALL EACH COLOR, A, B, AND C

TOTAL YARDAGE: 411 YARDS

GAUGE: 5 STITCHES = 1 INCH; 20 STITCHES = 4 INCHES

NEEDLE SIZE: US #7 (4.5MM) OR SIZE NEEDED TO OBTAIN GAUGE; US #5 (3.75MM) FOR RIBBING

SIZES: 0–3 MONTHS (3–6 MONTHS, 1 YEAR, 2 YEAR, 3 YEAR)

KNITTED MEASUREMENTS:
CIRCUMFERENCE: 14$\frac{1}{2}$″ (15″, 15$\frac{1}{2}$″, 16$\frac{1}{2}$″, 17$\frac{1}{2}$″)

Honestly, this pattern came about because our friend Petra had yarn left over when she knit *Max's First Cardigan* and she wanted a project to use up her extra yarn. She was a little tired of the double seed stitch and she thought it would look just as cute because of the matching colors. She was right.

PATTERN STITCH:

color B: work in garter stitch (all knit) for 2 rows

color C: work in St st for 6 rows

color B: work in garter stitch (all knit) for 2 rows

color A: work in St st for 6 rows

Repeat this pattern for entire hat.

With #5 needle and color A, cast on 72 (76, 80, 84, 88) stitches. Work in K2, P2 ribbing for 6 rows. Change to #7 needle and work in pattern until piece measures 5″ (5$\frac{1}{2}$″, 6″, 6$\frac{1}{2}$″, 6$\frac{1}{2}$″) from cast-on edge, ending on a WS row. Begin decreases as follows, making

sure to continue working in the pattern stitch:

ROW 1: *(K5, K2tog)* across row.

ROWS 2, 4, 6, 8: Work whatever row of the pattern stitch you are on without any decreases.

ROW 3: *(K4, K2tog)* across row.

ROW 5: *(K3, K2tog)* across row.

ROW 7: *(K2, K2tog)* across row.

ROW 9: *(K1, K2tog)* across row.

ROW 10: *(K2tog)* across row.

Cut yarn, leaving 20″. Thread yarn through remaining loops and sew down seam.

Make 3 tassels, 1 in each color, and attach.

baby it's you, for him

sugar and spice

Nancy had twins—a boy and a girl. Before they were born, Nancy was an avid knitter and had knitted each of them several sweaters and blankets. Since their arrival she obviously had a lot less time on her hands, but she still wanted to knit. Nancy decided that hats would be the perfect project. She made some simple roll hats. She loved them. She wanted to make more hats but at the same time she wanted a project that was a bit more challenging. We suggested she make this hat. Although the stitch was still simple stockinette, Nancy could learn a new knitting technique—intarsia. She was slightly intimidated by the idea of working with two colors at the same time but decided to bite the bullet and give it a try. Within a week, she had made a hat for Rachel and one for Avery, and she still managed to feed and bathe them!

YARN: FILATURA DI CROSA, PRIMO (77 YARDS / 50G BALL)

FIBER CONTENT: 100% ANTARCTIC WOOL

COLORS:
GIRL VERSION: A-7 (MAGENTA), B-2150 (ORANGE), C-261 (CHARTREUSE), D-3 (TEAL)
BOY VERSION: A-2151 (RED), B-238 (BLUE), C-307 (OCHRE), D-244 (PEA)

AMOUNT: 1 BALL EACH COLOR, A, B, C, AND D

TOTAL YARDAGE: 308 YARDS

GAUGE: 4 STITCHES = 1 INCH; 16 STITCHES = 4 INCHES

NEEDLE SIZE: US #9 (5.5MM) OR SIZE NEEDED TO OBTAIN GAUGE; US #5 (3.75MM) DOUBLE-POINTED OR CIRCULAR NEEDLES FOR I-CORDS

SIZES: 0–3 MONTHS (3–6 MONTHS, 1 YEAR, 2 YEAR, 3 YEAR)

KNITTED MEASUREMENTS: CIRCUMFERENCE: 14" (14$\frac{1}{2}$", 15", 16", 17") MAKE 2 SQUARES

With #9 needle, cast on 28 (30, 30, 32, 34) stitches: 14 (15, 15, 16, 17) in color A, 14 (15, 15, 16, 17) in color B. Work 8 rows of garter stitch as follows: Row 1: K 14 (15, 15, 16, 17) in color B, K14 (15, 15, 16, 17) in color A. Row 2: K 14 (15, 15, 16, 17) in color A, K14 (15, 15, 16, 17) in color B. Then, beginning with a purl row, work in St st until piece measures 3" (3$\frac{1}{2}$", 3$\frac{1}{2}$", 4", 4") above garter ridge.

NOTE: MAKE SURE THE SEAM IS ON THE OPPOSITE SIDE OF THE GARTER-STITCH SEAM.

Then switch to 14 (15, 15, 16, 17) stitches in color C and 14 (15, 15, 16, 17) in color D. Work 2" (2", 2$\frac{1}{2}$", 3", 3") in St st in these colors. Bind off all stitches loosely.

FINISHING:

Sew the top of the hat together. Sew down the side seams, turning up the garter border to make a brim.

With a #5 double-pointed or circular needle, cast on 3 stitches. Make an 8" I-cord in color A. Then make an identical I-cord in color B. Attach the I-cords to the top of the hat, attaching the cord made in color A to color C on the hat and the cord made in color B to color D on the hat.

sugar and spice, for her

ponchos &
dresses

As if there aren't already a million reasons you might want to knit for a baby girl . . . dresses and ponchos . . . need we say more? *Fuzzy Wuzzy Was a Poncho* is as simple as can be. It is the perfect project for beginners who just want to practice knitting. It is like knitting two scarves and then sewing them together. The crochet fuzzy border adds a bit of decadence and whimsy. Those who knit *The Princess's Poncho* will get plenty of practice increasing and decreasing as well as making tassels. *Dress Me Up* is a fun A-line swing dress. The colors are bright and cheery, and the frilly bottom just screams girly girl. Make it a little big so you can put a long-sleeved T-shirt underneath it and let your girl wear it through the fall. *You Are My Sunshine* is equally fun and feminine. The bottom of the dress is flouncy, and the top is a bit more tapered. You can't go wrong with any of the projects in this chapter.

fuzzy wuzzy was a poncho

Judith has three grandchildren for whom she is constantly knitting. One day she was baby-sitting for her youngest grandchild, Abigail, who was two at the time. Judith loves showing off Abigail, so she brought her into the store for a visit. Judith promised herself she would not buy anything. But Abigail, who already loves dress up, saw *Fuzzy Wuzzy Was a Poncho* and wanted to try it on—you could tell she felt like a princess in it. Well, it was quite a challenge convincing her to take it off. Needless to say, Judith did not leave the store empty-handed.

YARN: SCHAEFER YARNS, ELAINE (300 YARDS / 225G BALL); GEDIFRA, TECHNOHAIR (99 YARDS / 50G BALL)

FIBER CONTENT: ELAINE: 99% MERINO WOOL / 1% NYLON; TECHNOHAIR: 100% POLYAMIDE

COLORS: A: ELAINE-PEBBLES; B: TECHNOHAIR-9607

AMOUNT: 1 (2, 2) BALL(S) COLOR A; (1, 1) BALL COLOR B

TOTAL YARDAGE: 300 (600, 600) YARDS COLOR A; B: 99 YARDS COLOR B

GAUGE: 4 STITCHES = 1 INCH IN GARTER STITCH; 16 STITCHES = 4 INCHES IN GARTER STITCH

NEEDLE SIZE: US 10 (6MM) OR SIZE NEEDED TO OBTAIN GAUGE; J CROCHET HOOK

SIZES: 1 YEAR (2 YEAR, 3 YEAR)

KNITTED MEASUREMENTS: THIS REFLECTS THE MEASUREMENT OF THE KNITTED PIECES, NOT OF THE PONCHO ONCE IT IS SEWN TOGETHER. WIDTH = (11", 14", 15½"), LENGTH = 15" (17", 18½")

FRONT AND BACK:

(make 2 pieces)

With #10 needle and color A, cast on 44 (56, 62) stitches. Work in garter stitch until piece measures 15" (17", 18½") from cast-on edge. Bind off all stitches loosely.

FINISHING:

Sew together as shown in diagram below. With J crochet hook work 2 rows of single crochet around all edges in color B.

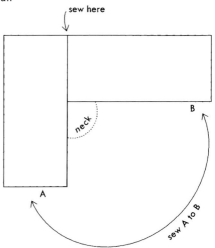

the princess's poncho

YARN: FILATURA DI CROSA, ZARA (137 YARDS / 50G BALL) AND CRYSTAL PALACE YARNS, FIZZ (120 YARDS / 50G BALL)

FIBER CONTENT: ZARA: 100% MERINO WOOL; FIZZ: 100% POLYESTER

COLORS: A: ZARA-1449, B: FIZZ-7225

AMOUNT: 6 (6, 9) BALLS COLOR A; 1 (1, 1) BALL COLOR B.

TOTAL YARDAGE: 816 (816, 1224) YARDS COLOR A; 120 (120, 120) YARDS COLOR B

GAUGE: 2 STITCHES = 1 INCH; 8 STITCHES = 4 INCHES

NEEDLE SIZE: US #17 (12MM) OR SIZE NEEDED TO OBTAIN GAUGE; N CROCHET HOOK

SIZES: 1 YEAR (2 YEAR, 3 YEAR)

Yarn is worked triple throughout the poncho—this means you should hold 3 strands of Zara together as though they are 1.

Who says five-year-olds don't know fashion? While shopping with her mom, Cleo saw a poncho and decided it was a must-have for her fall wardrobe. Her mom took one look at the price tag and suggested that maybe Cleo ought to ask her aunt Jordana to knit one for her instead. Unable to resist Cleo's charm, Jordana whipped this little number up over the weekend. Now Cleo is the envy of all the little princesses in her kindergarten class.

BACK AND FRONT: (make 2)

With #17 needle and 3 strands of color A, cast on 2 stitches. Work in garter stitch while increasing 1 stitch (knit into the front and the back) at each edge of every row until you have 38 (42, 50) stitches. Then begin decreasing 1 stitch (K2, K2tog) at the beginning only of every row until 14 (14, 16) stitches remain. Bind off loosely.

FINISHING:

Sew the front and the back of the poncho together from the top down the entire decrease edge. Make fringe using 4 strands of color B held together and attach it, spacing it evenly around the poncho at intervals of approximately 1″. With 3 strands of color A, work 1 row single crochet and 1 row shrimp stitch around the neck edge.

dress me up

Jennifer and her family were going to a wedding with her college crowd. Since college she has had the reputation of not being very domestic. This doesn't usually bother her, but she felt like proving her friends wrong and showing off her new knitting skills. None of her college friends believed she could knit anything decent, so she came to us for help. She wanted to knit a dress for her daughter to wear at the wedding. We looked through books and books, but most patterns seemed too complicated or she just didn't care for them. Jordana wrote this pattern for her—a simple A-line with a great fuzzy, colorful accent. Needless to say, Jennifer's friends were more than impressed. She and her daughter got more compliments than the bride.

BACK AND FRONT: (make 2)

With #8 needle and 2 strands of color C, cast on 72 (78, 84) stitches. Work in garter stitch for 2″. Change to color A and work in St st for 8 rows. Then decrease 1 stitch at each end every 4th row 10 (11, 12) times until 52 (56, 60) stitches remain. Then decrease 1 stitch at each end of every other row 5 (4, 3) times until 42 (48, 54) stitches remain.

NOTE: DECREASES SHOULD BE WORKED AS FOLLOWS: K2, SSK, K TO LAST 4 STITCHES, K2TOG, K2. WHEN PIECE MEASURES 12″ (13½″, 15″) FROM CAST-ON EDGE, ENDING WITH A WS ROW.

Shape Armholes: Bind off 3 stitches at the beginning of the next 2 rows. Bind off 2 stitches at the beginning of the next 2 rows. Then decrease 1 stitch at each edge of every other row 2 (3, 3) times until you have 28 (32, 38) stitches. (See step-by-step instructions.) Continue to work in St st until piece measures 16″ (17½″, 19″) from cast-on edge, ending with a WS row.

Shape Neck: Bind off center 10 stitches. Working each side of neck separately, at the beginning of each neck edge, every other row, bind off 3 stitches 0 (1, 1) time, bind off 2 stitches 1 time, 1 stitch 2 times until you have 5 (4, 7) stitches. (See step-by-step instructions.) Continue working on remaining 5 (4, 7) stitches until piece measures 18″ (19½″, 21″) from cast-on edge, ending with a WS row. Bind off remaining stitches loosely.

YARN: S. CHARLES, VICTORIA (72 YARDS / 50G BALL) AND CRYSTAL PALACE YARNS, FIZZ (120 YARDS / 50G BALL)

FIBER CONTENT: VICTORIA: 60% COTTON; 40% VISCOSE; FIZZ: 100% POLYESTER

COLORS: A: VICTORIA-39; B: VICTORIA-21; C: FIZZ-7223

AMOUNT: 4 (4, 5) BALLS COLOR A; 1 (1, 1) BALL COLOR B; 2 (2, 2) BALLS COLOR C

TOTAL YARDAGE: VICTORIA 360 (360, 432) YARDS; FIZZ 240 (240, 240) YARDS

GAUGE: 4½ STITCHES = 1 INCH; 18 STITCHES = 4 INCHES

NEEDLE SIZE: US #8 (5MM) OR SIZE NEEDED TO OBTAIN GAUGE; H CROCHET HOOK

SIZES: 1 YEAR (2 YEAR, 3 YEAR)

KNITTED MEASUREMENTS: CHEST WIDTH = 9½″ (10½″, 13″), LENGTH = 18″ (19½″, 21″)

FINISHING:

Sew shoulder seams together. Sew up side seam. With H crochet hook and color B, work 1 row of single crochet around each armhole edge and around neck.

STEP-BY-STEP GUIDE TO SHAPING THE ARMHOLES

ROW 1: Bind off 3 stitches. Knit to the end of the row. Turn work.

ROW 2: Bind off 3 stitches. Purl to the end of the row. Turn work.

ROW 3: Bind off 2 stitches. Knit to the end of the row. Turn work.

ROW 4: Bind off 2 stitches. Purl to the end of the row. Turn work.

ROW 5: K2, SSK, knit to last 4 stitches, K2tog, K2. Turn work.

ROW 6: Purl. Turn work.

Repeat rows 5 and 6 1 (2, 2) more time(s).

Remember that after binding off the center stitches, you will work one side at a time.

ROW 1: Knit 11 (13, 16) stitches; with the 10th (12th, 15th) stitch, begin to bind off the center 10 stitches. For example, for the 1-year size, this means you should pull the 10th stitch over the 11th stitch, and this is your first bind-off. When you are done binding off the center 10 stitches, check to make sure you have 9 (11, 14) stitches on each side of the hole, including the stitch on the right-hand needle. Knit to end of row. Turn work.

ROW 2: Purl. Turn work.

If you are making the 1-year size, skip to row 5. Otherwise, continue in sequence.

ROW 3: Bind off first 3 stitches. Knit to end of row. Turn work.

ROW 4: Purl. Turn work.

ROW 5: Bind off first 2 stitches. Knit to end of row. Turn work.

ROW 6: Purl. Turn work.

ROW 7: Bind off 1 stitch. Knit to end of row. Turn work.

ROW 8: Purl. Turn work.

ROW 9: Bind off 1 stitch. Knit to end of row. Turn work.

ROW 10: Purl.

• For the other side of the neck edge, attach yarn to the remaining stitches and begin binding off 3 stitches immediately (or 2 stitches, if you are making the 1-year size). You will now be binding off when you are purling. Finish neck shaping as on other side and bind off remaining stitches.

• When you are done with the bind-off instructions, compare the length of the front piece to the length of the back. If the front and back measure the same, bind off the remaining stitches. If the front is too short, continue knitting and purling until the pieces are of equal length, then bind off.

you are my sunshine

Deena wanted to make something special for her daughter Rena to wear during the holidays. She wanted it to be whimsical and very girly. She decided on this dress because the combination of Cancun's texture and Clip's array of colors fit the bill perfectly. The dress can be made in many yarn variations— for example, using a textured yarn in place of the Cancun and a flat for the Clip. However, if you want something a little less flashy but still like the shape of the dress, it looks great in two solid, flat colors too.

YARN: S. CHARLES, CANCUN (93 YARDS / 50G BALL); KLAUS KOLLECTION, CLIP (182 YARDS / 100G BALL)

FIBER CONTENT: CANCUN: 68% POLY-ESTER, 14% VISCOSE, 10% POLYAMIDE, 8% COTTON; CLIP: 100% COTTON

COLORS: A: CANCUN-70; B: CLIP-159

AMOUNT: 3 (4, 4) BALLS COLOR A; 2 (2, 3) BALLS COLOR B

TOTAL YARDAGE: 279 (372, 372) YARDS COLOR A; 364 (364, 549) YARDS COLOR B

GAUGE: 5 STITCHES = 1 INCH; 20 STITCHES = 4 INCHES

NEEDLE SIZE: US #6 (4MM) OR SIZE NEEDED TO OBTAIN GAUGE; G CROCHET WORK

SIZES: 1 YEAR (2 YEAR, 3 YEAR)

KNITTED MEASUREMENTS: CHEST WIDTH = 10" (11, 12"), LENGTH = 17½" (20", 22")

STRIPE PATTERN:

Work in St st as follows:

4 rows color A

2 rows color B

BACK AND FRONT: (make 2)

With #6 needle and color B, cast on 100 (112, 120) stitches. Work in garter stitch (all knit) for 10 rows. Begin working in striped pattern until piece measures 11½" (13¼", 14¾") from cast-on edge, ending with a WS row of color B. **Decrease Row:** K2tog across row until 50 (56, 60) stitches remain. Continue in St st with only color B for 1¼" more, ending with a WS row. **Shape Armholes:** When piece measures 12¾" (14½", 16"), bind off 3 stitches at the beginning of the next 2 rows, 2 stitches at the beginning of the following 2 rows, and 1 stitch at each end of the next and every other row 5 times until you have 30 (36, 40) stitches. (See step-by-step instructions.) When piece measures 14½" (17", 19") from cast-on edge, ending on a WS row **Shape Neck:** Bind off center 8 stitches. Working each side of neck separately, bind off at neck edge 3 stitches 1 time, 2 stitches 1 time, 1 stitch 2 (3, 3) times. (See step-by-step instructions.) Continue on remaining 4 (6, 8) stitches until piece measures 17½" (20", 22"). Bind off remaining stitches loosely.

FINISHING:

Sew shoulder and side seams together. With G crochet hook, work 1 row single crochet around all edges. Then work 1 row of picot crochet around all borders as follows: *Single crochet into 2 stitches, chain 3, single crochet into first chain*, repeat from start.

STEP-BY-STEP GUIDE TO SHAPING THE ARMHOLES

ROW 1: Bind off 3 stitches. Knit to the end of the row. Turn work.

ROW 2: Bind off 3 stitches. Purl to the end of the row. Turn work.

ROW 3: Bind off 2 stitches. Knit to the end of the row. Turn work.

ROW 4: Bind off 2 stitches. Purl to the end of the row. Turn work.

ROW 5: K2, SSK, knit to last 4 stitches, K2tog, K2. Turn work.

ROW 6: Purl. Turn work.

Repeat rows 5 and 6 4 (4, 4) more times.

STEP-BY-STEP GUIDE TO SHAPING THE NECK

Remember that after binding off the center stitches, you will work one side at a time.

ROW 1: Knit 13 (16, 18) stitches; with the 12th (15th, 17th) stitch, begin to bind off the center 8 stitches. For example, for the 1-year size, this means you should pull the 12th stitch over the 13th stitch, and this is your first bind-off. When you are done binding off the center 8 stitches, check to make sure you have 11 (14, 16) stitches on each side of the hole, including the stitch on the right-hand needle. Knit to end of row. Turn work.

ROW 2: Purl. Turn work.

ROW 3: Bind off first 3 stitches. Knit to end of row. Turn work.

ROW 4: Purl. Turn work.

ROW 5: Bind off first 2 stitches. Knit to end of row. Turn work.

ROW 6: Purl. Turn work.

ROW 7: Bind off 1 stitch. Knit to end of row. Turn work.

ROW 8: Purl. Turn work.

Repeat rows 7 and 8 1 (2, 2) more time(s).

• For the other side of the neck edge, attach yarn to the remaining stitches and begin binding off 3 stitches immediately. You will now be binding off when you are purling. Finish neck shaping as on other side and bind off remaining stitches.

• When you are done with the bind-off instructions, compare the length of the front piece to the length of the back. If the front and back measure the same, bind off the remaining stitches. If the front is too short, continue knitting and purling until the pieces are of equal length, then bind off.

blankets &
bunting

All babies need at least one blanket that is soft and cuddly. Although baby blankets are a larger undertaking than sweaters and hats, they are longer lasting and involve minimal finishing. And the best part: babies never outgrow them. Sometimes they even take their much-loved baby blankets to college with them.

We've included four quick-to-knit snuggly baby blankets here. *How Tara's Scarf Became a Blanket* is worked on a #19 needle and uses just the knit stitch. It combines four colors, which really affords the knitter some creativity despite the simplicity. We chose to knit one of the blankets in a soft pastel combination and the other in a bold palette of primaries, but the possibilities for color combinations are truly endless. *Barbara's Blanket* is also a super-fast and easy knit. It requires the knitter to follow a straightforward two-row pattern; one row is all knit, while the other has a combination of knits and purls. *Super Shower Gift* is a fun introduction to stripes. Picking the colors for this blanket is half the fun. We've seen many wonderful combinations over the years, and they all look great—from the traditional ones to the super-funky and frankly psychedelic ones.

Building Blocks is a traditional baby blanket pattern, but we made it a little more distinctive by knitting it in two colors of cotton chenille. We still used rather traditional blues and pinks for our blankets, but we have seen it knit in dozens of fun combinations—for example, green and yellow make a perfect spring-looking unisex blanket. And purple and lime green looked great too. This blanket is also the most challenging of the four. It requires the knitter to follow a 24-row pattern (albeit a simple one) that uses the knit and purl stitch in the same row. A row counter and stitch markers are helpful accessories when knitting this blanket.

Buntings are also a great baby project. They are warm and snuggly, making them perfect for baby's ride home from the hospital. They used to fill the pages of pattern books of yesteryear. However, if you followed one of them for today's babies, you would be in for a shock when you realize the baby can't be strapped into a car seat or carriage when wearing a bunting. Jordana discovered this problem after making an old-fashioned bunting for her son. Her frustration led her to cut a hole in her bunting, which then led us to design *Frustration Is the Mother of Invention*. This modern bunting has a hole in the center of both sides so all the straps and harnesses that keep our babies safe are compatible with it.

how tara's
scarf
became
a blanket

YARN: FILATURA DI CROSA, ZARA (137 YARDS / 50G BALL)

FIBER CONTENT: 100% MERINO WOOL

COLORS:
GIRL VERSION: A-1474 (YELLOW), B-1527 (GREEN), C-1472 (BLUE), D-1510 (PINK)
BOY VERSION: A-1704 (TURQUOISE), B-1509 (YELLOW), C-1449 (RED), D-1500 (BLUE)

AMOUNT: 3 BALLS OF EACH COLOR: A, B, C, AND D

TOTAL YARDAGE: 1,644 YARDS

GAUGE: 2 STITCHES = 1 INCH; 8 STITCHES = 4 INCHES

NEEDLE SIZE: CIRCULAR 32" US #19 (15MM) OR SIZE NEEDED TO OBTAIN GAUGE

KNITTED MEASUREMENT: 25" X 30"

Yarn is worked quadruple throughout the blanket—this means you should hold 1 strand of each color, A, B, C, and D, and work them together as though they are 1. We suggest you roll the 4 colors together.

Tara made lots of scarves. Her favorite was a simple garter-stitch pattern made with 4 strands of Zara knit on a #19 needle. She casted on 12 stitches, knit, and zippity-doo-dah—she had a great-looking scarf in less than two hours! After a while, Tara had made one for nearly everyone she knew. Then all of a sudden it seemed that everyone she knew was having a baby. Tara decided to turn her favorite scarf pattern into her favorite baby blanket pattern. She chose several colorways—pastels, brights, and a few funky color combinations for her downtown friends. Within a few weeks, she had made five blankets like this and was thrilled. Her friends loved the blankets and Tara, delighted with her new design, filled up another basket with yarn to make a few more.

With #19 needle and 4 strands of Zara, cast on 50 stitches. Work in garter stitch until piece measures 30". Bind off loosely.

FRINGE:

Cut 10" lengths of all colors. Using 1 strand of each color, attach fringe at top and bottom of blanket, spacing it as desired.

barbara's blanket

YARN: SKACEL, NO KIDDING (88 YARDS / 200G BALL)

FIBER CONTENT: 100% ACRYLIC

COLORS:
GIRL VERSION: 335
BOY VERSION: 75

AMOUNT: 2 BALLS

TOTAL YARDAGE: 176 YARDS

GAUGE: 1.1 STITCHES = 1 INCH; 6 STITCHES = 4 INCHES

NEEDLE SIZE: CIRCULAR 32" US #17 (12MM) OR SIZE NEEDED TO OBTAIN GAUGE

KNITTED MEASUREMENT: 30" X 30"

Barbara has been making this blanket as her signature baby gift for years. She loves it because it knits up in a flash, the pattern is so very simple, the yarn is soft, and there is no finishing. (Barbara hates finishing. Whenever she makes a sweater, she sends the pieces to her friend in Israel to put it together for her!) Jordana had always been a wee bit skeptical about this blanket. She wasn't sure the yarn was right for a baby blanket. She thought it might be too thick and too fuzzy. So when Barbara gave Jordana this blanket as a gift for her son, Max, Jordana was secretly a little disappointed. But now this is Max's most used, most wonderful blanket, and Jordana is a convert—she LOVES the blanket. Max was born in December 2002, at the beginning of a freezing cold winter, and he never *ever* went out without Barbara's blanket covering him to keep him toasty warm in the stroller.

With #17 needle, cast on 34 stitches. Work 8 rows in garter stitch. Then work in pattern as follows: Row 1: Knit. Row 2: K6, purl 22, K6. Repeat rows 1 and 2 until blanket measures 28" from cast-on edge. Work 8 rows in garter stitch. Bind off all stitches loosely.

super shower gift

This is Karen's standard baby shower gift. She loves making it for a ton of reasons. Just to name a few: the yarn is super-soft, the pattern is super-easy, it knits up super-quick—and, best of all, everyone attending the shower thinks she is super-talented. It is worked in a simple garter stitch—but the stripes make it a little different. You never want to put your knitting down when making stripes because you always want to get to the next color, and the more you do the better it looks.

YARN: GEDIFRA, NEW AGE (115 YARDS / 50G BALL)

FIBER CONTENT: 100% POLYAMID

COLORS:
GIRL VERSION: A-2106, B-2149, C-2104
BOY VERSION: A-2183, B-2184, C-2104

AMOUNT: 5 BALLS COLOR A; 4 BALLS COLOR B; 3 BALLS COLOR C

TOTAL YARDAGE: 1,380 YARDS

GAUGE: 2½ STITCHES = 1 INCH; 10 STITCHES = 4 INCHES

NEEDLE SIZE: CIRCULAR 24" OR 32" US #13 (9MM) OR SIZE NEEDED TO OBTAIN GAUGE

KNITTED MEASUREMENT: 30" X 30"

Yarn is worked double throughout the blanket—this means you should hold 2 strands of yarn together as though they are 1.

With #13 needle and 2 strands of color A, cast on 76 stitches. Work in garter stitch pattern as follows: 8 rows color A; 4 rows color B; 2 rows color C; 4 rows color B. Repeat this sequence until piece measures approximately 28", ending with 8 rows of color A. Bind off loosely.

FINISHING:

With #13 needle and color A, pick up 1 stitch on side edges between each garter ridge. Work 8 rows in garter stitch and bind off loosely.

building blocks

Our accountant, Len, loves this blanket. Several years ago, Len was at our store and asked if we could knit a blanket for a friend of his who was having a baby in a few weeks. We showed him a few options, and he chose this one. Len liked the softness of the chenille, its weight, and the wide array of colors from which he could choose. Len didn't know which sex the baby was going to be, so he chose a yellow and green combination. The blanket was a big hit, and only weeks later Len wanted another one for a different friend. Since then, this has become the gift all his friends expect. We've made some for him in great color combos—soft pastels like baby pink or baby blue and off-white or bold primary colors such as red and yellow or red and electric blue. Once we did a white-off-white combination that was understated but beautiful.

YARN: CRYSTAL PALACE YARNS, COTTON CHENILLE (100 YARDS / 50G BALL)

FIBER CONTENT: 100% COTTON

COLORS:
GIRL VERSION: 5509 AND 1109
BOY VERSION: 2214 AND 5638

AMOUNT: 5 BALLS COLOR A; 5 BALLS COLOR B

TOTAL YARDAGE: 1,000 YARDS

GAUGE: 2½ STITCHES = 1 INCH; 10 STITCHES = 4 INCHES

NEEDLE SIZE: CIRCULAR 24" OR 32" US #11 (8MM) OR SIZE NEEDED TO OBTAIN GAUGE

KNITTED MEASUREMENT: 30" X 30"

Yarn is worked double throughout the blanket—this means you should hold 1 strand of color A with 1 strand of color B and work them together as though they are 1.

With #11 needle and 2 strands of yarn, cast on 80 stitches. Work 10 rows in garter stitch. Then work box pattern as follows:

ROWS 1–12: K10, *(K10, P10)* 3 times, K10.

ROWS 13–24: K10, *(P10, K10)* 3 times, K10.

Repeat rows 1–24 until the blanket measures approximately 28". End with either row 12 or row 24. Then work 10 rows in garter stitch and bind off loosely.

frustration is the mother of invention

Before Jordana knew that Max was going to be a boy, she had the desire to knit for her baby. She wanted to make something unisex. A bunting seemed like the perfect project. The baby-to-be was going to be born in late December and would surely need something extra-warm. Jordana knit a bunting in an oatmeal color, and once she found out she was having a boy she chose a denim blue color for the ribbing. Max was born on December 24. After a few weeks, Jordana was eager to get outside and put Max in his bunting. The only problem was that he could not wear it in the Baby Bjorn because the bunting did not have legs and he could not wear it in the car seat carrier, which had a strap that came up between his legs. Frustrated, Jordana wondered what to do—she wanted Max to be able to wear the bunting outdoors; otherwise, what was the point? Aha! She cut a hole on either side of the bunting so the strap could slide through it. This pattern is written so you won't have to cut a hole in the bunting; the hole is written into it as a cast-off and -on in the center of the back and front pieces.

BACK:

With #8 needle and color A, cast on 64 stitches. Work in garter stitch until piece measures 5¹/₂″ from cast-on edge. Next row: Bind off center 6 stitches, knit to end. (See step-by-step instructions.) Next row: Knit to bound-off stitches, then cast on 6 stitches in center of row, knit to end. Continue working in garter stitch until piece measures 16″ from cast-on edge. **Shape Armhole:** Bind off 5 stitches at the beginning of the next 2 rows. (See step-by-step instructions.) Continue in garter stitch on remaining 54 stitches until piece measures 21″ from cast-on edge. Bind off all stitches loosely.

FRONT:

Work as for back until piece measures 8″ from cast-on edge. (Don't forget to bind off and cast on the center 6 stitches at 5¹/₂″.) **Split work in 2:** Bind off the center 4 stitches and continue to work in garter stitch, working each side separately, until piece measures 16″ from cast-on edge. **Shape Armhole:** Bind off 5 stitches at outside edge of work. Continue to work in garter stitch on remaining 25 stitches until piece measures 19″ from cast-on edge, ending with a WS row. (See step-by-step instructions.) **Shape Neck:** At beginning of each neck edge in every other row, bind of 5 stitches 1 time, bind off 3 stitches 1 time, 2 stitches 1 time, 1

stitch 2 times. (See step-by-step instructions.) Continue working in garter stitch on remaining 13 stitches until piece measures 21″ from cast-on edge. Bind off all remaining stitches loosely.

SLEEVES:

With #6 needle and color B, cast on 30 stitches. Work in K1, P1 ribbing for 1¹/₄″. Increase 6 stitches evenly across the last row of ribbing. Change to #8 needle and color A; work in garter stitch. **AT THE SAME TIME,** increase 1 stitch at each end every 8th row 7 times until you have 44 stitches.

NOTE: INCREASE LEAVING 2 EDGE STITCHES ON EITHER SIDE OF WORK. THIS MEANS YOU SHOULD KNIT 2 STITCHES, INCREASE 1 STITCH, KNIT TO THE LAST 2 STITCHES, INCREASE 1 STITCH, AND THEN KNIT THE REMAINING 2 STITCHES. INCREASING LIKE THIS MAKES IT EASIER TO SEW UP YOUR SEAMS.

When sleeve measures 6¹/₂″ from cast-on edge, ending on a WS row, bind off all stitches loosely.

HOOD:

With #8 needle and color A, cast on 30 stitches. Work in garter stitch until piece measures 15″. Bind off all stitches loosely.

YARN: FILATURA DI CROSA, ZARA (137 YARDS / 50G BALL)

FIBER CONTENT: 100% MERINO WOOL

COLORS: A-1527; B-1474

AMOUNT: 7 SKEINS COLOR A; 1 SKEIN COLOR B

TOTAL YARDAGE: 1,096 YARDS

GAUGE: 4¹/₂ STITCHES = 1 INCH; 18 STITCHES = 4 INCHES

NEEDLE SIZE: US #8 (5MM) OR SIZE NEEDED TO OBTAIN GAUGE FOR BODY, US #6 (4MM) FOR RIBBING

SIZES: 0–6 MONTHS

KNITTED MEASUREMENTS: WIDTH = 14″, LENGTH = 21″, SLEEVE LENGTH = 6¹/₂″

OTHER MATERIALS: 7 BUTTONS

FINISHING:

Sew shoulder seams together. Sew sleeves to body. Sew up side and sleeve seams. Fold hood in half and sew down 1 side, making a back seam. Sew the hood to the body.

Button band: With #6 needle and color B, pick up 50 stitches and work in K1, P1 ribbing for 6 rows.

Buttonhole band: With #6 needle and color B, pick up 50 stitches. Work 2 rows in K1, P1 ribbing. Buttonhole row: Rib 3, *(YO, Rib 2tog, rib 5)* 6 times, K2tog, YO, rib 3.

Hood ribbing: Pick up 74 stitches around front of hood and work in K1, P1 ribbing for 6 rows. Bind off all stitches loosely. Sew edge of hood ribbing to top of button band.

STEP-BY-STEP GUIDE TO BINDING OFF THE CENTER STITCHES

ROW 1: Knit 31 stitches; with the 30th stitch, begin to bind off the center 6 stitches. This means you should pull the 30th stitch over the 31st stitch, and this is your first bind-off. When you are done binding off the center 6 stitches, check to make sure you have 29 stitches on each side of the hole, including the stitch on the right-hand needle. Knit to end.

ROW 2: Knit 29 stitches. Cast 6 stitches back onto the needle. Knit 29 stitches.

STEP-BY-STEP GUIDE TO SHAPING THE ARMHOLES

ROW 1: Bind off 5 stitches. Knit to end. Turn work.

ROW 2: Bind off 5 stitches. Knit to end. Turn work.

STEP-BY-STEP GUIDE TO SHAPING THE NECK

ROW 1: Bind off 5 stitches. Knit to end. Turn work.

ROW 2: Knit. Turn work.

ROW 3: Bind off 3 stitches. Knit to end. Turn work.

ROW 4: Knit. Turn work.

ROW 5: Bind off 2 stitches. Knit to end. Turn work.

ROW 6: Knit. Turn work.

ROW 7: Bind off 1 stitch. Knit to end. Turn work.

ROW 8: Knit. Turn work.

Repeat rows 7 and 8 once more.

• When you are done with the bind-off instructions, compare the length of the front piece to the length of the back. If the front and the back measure the same, bind off the remaining stitches.

resources

Yarns used in this book can be ordered directly through The Yarn Company. However, yarns change seasonally and it is possible that some of the yarns may not be available when you are ready to place an order. Be flexible; you don't have to use the exact yarns used in a given pattern in order to get great results. Just choose a yarn or combination of yarns that achieve the required gauge. You can also contact the manufacturer for local dealers; many have helpful websites with this type of information.

The following is a list of all the manufacturers whose yarns were used in this book:

THE YARN COMPANY
2274 Broadway
New York, NY 10024
www.theyarnco.com

BLUE SKY ALPACA YARNS
BLUE SKY ALPACAS, INC.
P.O. Box 387
St. Francis, MN 55070
(888) 460-8862
www.blueskyalpacas.com

CRYSTAL PALACE YARNS
CRYSTAL PALACE
2320 Bissell Avenue
Richmond, CA 94804
(800) 666-7455
www.straw.com

**FILATURA DI CROSA &
TAHKI YARNS**
TAHKI/STACY CHARLES, INC.
8000 Cooper Avenue, Building #1
Glendale, NY 11385
(800) 338-9276
www.tahkistacycharles.com

KOIGU YARNS
KOIGU WOOL DESIGNS
563295 Glenelg/Holland Twnl Road
RR#1
Williamsford, Ontario N0H2V0
CANADA
(888) 765-WOOL
www.koigu.com

LANG YARNS
BERROCO YARNS
14 Elmdale Road, P.O. Box 367
Uxbridge, MA 01569
(800) 343-4948
www.berroco.com

**MANOS DEL URUGUAY
YARNS**
DESIGN SOURCE
38 Montvale Avenue, Suite 145
Stoneham, MA 02180
(888) 566-9970

MISSION FALLS YARNS
UNIQUE KOLOURS LTD.
28 North Bacton Hill Road
Malvern, PA 19355
(800) 252-3934
www.uniquekolours.com

**NORO, GEDIFRA & KLAUS
KOCH KOLLECTION**
KNITTING FEVER/EURO YARNS
P.O. Box 502
Roosevelt, NY 11575
(800) 645-3457
www.knittingfever.com

PRISM YARNS
PRISM ARTS, INC.
2595 30th Avenue North
St. Petersburg, FL 33713
(727) 327-3100

SCHAEFER YARNS
SCHAEFER YARN CO., LTD.
3514 Kelly's Corners Road
Interlaken, NY 14847
(800) 367-9276
www.schafferyarn.com

**ZITON YARN, SKACEL
YARN**
SKACEL COLLECTION, INC.
P.O. Box 88110
Seattle, WA 98138
(800) 255-1278
www.skacelknitting.com

index

Page numbers in *italics* indicate illustrations.

about the authors

Inveterate knitters since college, JULIE CARLES and JORDANA JACOBS left their respective careers in the medical and legal worlds to assume ownership of The Yarn Company, New York City's landmark knitting store, in 1997. The store has become a destination for celebrities and locals alike, who come for the quickly sold-out classes, unrivaled yarn selection, customized knitting patterns—and friendly conversation. The Yarn Company can be reached on the Web at www.theyarnco.com. Julie and Jordana live in New York City. They are the authors of *The Yarn Girls' Guide to Simple Knits.*